Women at War Work
1914-18

THE MANUFACTURE OF 4.5-INCH CARTRIDGE CASES:
OPERATING THE DRAWING PRESS

Women at War Work 1914-18

Two Views of British Women Engaged in
Supplying the Allied Effort
During the Great War

The Woman's Part

L. K. Yates

Carry On: British Women's Work in Wartime

LEONAUR

Women at War Work 1914-18
Two Views of British Women Engaged in Supplying the Allied Effort
During the Great War
The Woman's Part
by L. K. Yates
and
Carry On: British Women's Work in Wartime

First published under the titles
The Woman's Part
and
Carry On: British Women's Work in Wartime.

Leonaur is an imprint of Oakpast Ltd
Copyright in this form © 2012 Oakpast Ltd

ISBN: 978-0-85706-892-7 (hardcover)
ISBN: 978-0-85706-893-4 (softcover)

http://www.leonaur.com

Publisher's Notes

The views expressed in this book are not necessarily
those of the publisher.

Contents

CHAPTER 1

The Advent of Women in
Engineering Trades

In a period of titanic events it is difficult to characterize a single group of happenings as of special significance, yet at the end of the war it is likely that Great Britain will look back to the transformation of her home industries for war purposes as one of the greatest feats she has ever accomplished. The arousing of a nation to fight to the death for the principle of Liberty is doubtless one of the most stirring of spectacles in the human drama; it has repeated itself throughout history; but it has been left to this century to witness in the midst of such an upheaval the complete reorganization of a nation's industry, built up slowly and painfully by a modern civilization for its material support and utility.

Before the outbreak of hostilities Great Britain was supplying the world with the products of her workshops, but these products were mainly those needed by nations at peace. The coal mines of Northumberland, the foundries of the Midlands, the cotton mills of Lancashire were aiding vast populations in their daily human struggle, but the demand of 1914 for vast requirements for war purposes found Great Britain unprepared. The instantaneous rearrangement of industries for war purposes, possible to Germany by reason of forty years of stealthy war preparations, was out of the question for a nation that neither contemplated nor prepared for a European conflagration. Eight or nine months had to elapse before the people of Great Britain were aroused to the realities of modern warfare.

It was then only that a large public became aware that the Herculean struggle was not merely a conflict between armies and navies, but between British science and German science, between British chemists and German chemists, between British workshops and the workshops of Germany. The realization of these facts led to the creation of the Ministry of Munitions in May 1915 and the rapid rearrangement of industries and industrial conditions. Before the war, three national factories in Great Britain were sufficient to fulfil the demand for output for possible war purposes; today, (as at time of first publication), there are more than 150 national factories and over 5,000 controlled establishments, scattered up and down the country, all producing munitions of war. The whole of the North Country and the whole of the Midlands have, in fact, become a vast arsenal.

Standing on an eminence in the North, one may by day watch ascending the smoke of from 400 to 500 munition factories, and by night at many a point in the Midland counties one may survey an encircling zone of flames as they belch forth from the chimneys of the engineering works of war. The vast majority of these workshops had previously to the war never produced a gun, a shell, or a cartridge. Today, (as at time of first publication), makers of agricultural and textile machinery are engaged on munitions, producers of lead pencils are turning out shrapnel; a manufacturer of gramophones is producing fuses; a court jeweller is engaged in the manufacture of optical instruments; a maker of cream separators has now an output of primers. Nor is this all. New industries have been started and languishing trades have been revived.

The work of reorganization has been prodigious, and when the history of Britain's share in the war comes to be written in the leisured days of peace, it is unlikely that the record will transmit to a future generation how much effort it has taken to produce the preponderance in munitions now achieved. With the huge task of securing an adequate supply of raw material has gone hand in hand the production of a sufficiency of suitable machinery and machine tools, the equipment of laboratories for chemical research, the erection, or adaptation, of accommodation in which to house the new 'plant', and the supply of a continuous stream of suitable labour. In face of the growing needs of the navy and army this labour question has been a crucial test; it is a testimony to the 'will to win' of the whole people that the problem from the outset has found its solution. As soon as the importance of the demand for munitions workers was widely understood, a supply of labour has continuously streamed into the factory gates. There are now 2,000,000 persons employed in munitions industries—exclusive of Admiralty work—of which one-third are women.

The advent of the women in the engineering shops and their success in a group of fresh trades may be accounted as an omen of deep significance. Women in this country have, it is true, taken their place in factory life from the moment that machinery swept away the spinning-wheel from the domestic hearth, and it is more often the woman mill-hand, or factory 'lass', who is the wealthier partner in many a Lancashire home. Women before the war, to be sure, took part in factory life where such commodities as textiles, clothing, food, household goods, &c., were produced, but by consensus of opinion—feminine as well as masculine—her presence in engineering works, save on mere routine work, or on a few delicate processes, was considered in the pre-war period as unsuitable and undesirable.

SHARING A COMMON TASK

At the outbreak of hostilities, a few of the most far-sighted employers, contemplating a shortage of labour through the recruitment of men for military service, hazarded the opinion that women might be employed on all kinds of simple repetition work in the engineering shops. Further than that even the optimist did not go. There was also no indication that women would be willing to adventure into a world where long hours and night-work prevailed, from which evils they were protected in the days of peace by stringent Factory Acts. Events have proved that the women of Great Britain are as ready as their menfolk to sacrifice comfort and personal convenience to the demands of a great cause, and as soon as it was made known that their services were required, they came forward in their hundreds of thousands.

They have come from the office and the shop, from domestic service and the dressmaker's room, from the high schools and the colleges, and from the quietude of the stately homes of the leisured rich. They have travelled from far-off corners in the United Kingdom as well as from homesteads in Australia and New Zealand, and from lonely farms in South Africa and Canada. Every stratum of society has provided its share of willing women workers eager from one cause or another to 'do their bit'.

Even in the early days of the advent of women in the munitions shops, I have seen working together, side by side, the daughter of an earl, a shopkeeper's widow, a graduate from Girton, a domestic servant and a young woman from a lonely farm in Rhodesia, whose husband had joined the colours. Social status, so stiff a barrier in this country

9

in pre-war days, was forgotten in the factory, as in the trenches, and they were all working together as happily as the members of a united family.

Employers and former employees likewise often share a common task in the workshops of the war. At Woolwich, for example, a lady of delicate upbringing could, at one period, have been seen arriving at the Arsenal in the early hours of each morning, accompanied by her former maid, both being the while 'hands' in the employ of the State. It is well known in certain circles how Lady Scott, the widow of the famous Antarctic explorer, put aside all private interests to take up work in a munitions factory, how Lady Gertrude Crawford became an official, supervising women's work in shipyards, and how Lady Mary Hamilton (later Mrs. Kenyon Slaney), the eldest daughter of the Duke of Abercorn, and Miss Stella Drummond, daughter of General Drummond, have won distinction as workers in 'advanced' processes of munitions production.

These are but a few distinguished names amongst a crowd of women of all degrees of society who have achieved unexpected success in work to which they were entirely unaccustomed. Amongst this nameless multitude, attention has been called from time to time to the remarkable feats in the engineering and chemical trades, in electrical works, and in the shipyards, of kitchen-maids and of dressmakers, of governesses and children's nurses.

The underlying motives, all actuated by war conditions, which have turned the tide of women's work into new and unfamiliar occupations, are, however, more diverse than is generally supposed. Unquestionably, the two main driving forces have been patriotism and economic pressure, and of these patriotism, the love of country, the pride of Empire, accounts for a large proportion of women recruits. Yet there are other motives at work: the old human forces of family love and self-sacrifice, pride, anger, hatred, and even humour. I have questioned workers at the lathes and in doping rooms, in Filling Factories, and in wood-workers' shops, and find the mass of new labour in the munitions works is there from distinctive individual reasons. It is only by the recognition of all these forces that successful management of a new factor in the labour problem is possible. An indication of the life-history of one or two individual munitions workers may exemplify the point.

There is the case of a girl tool-setter in a factory near London. She is the only child of an old army family. When war broke out, she realized that for the first time in many generations her family could send no representative to fight the country's battles. Her father was an old man, long past military age. The girl, although in much request at home, took up work in a base hospital in France, but at the end of a year, when broken down from over-strain, was ordered six months' rest in England. Recovery followed in two months, and again, spurred by the thought of inaction in a time of national peril, she entered a munitions factory as an ordinary employee. After nine months' work she had only lost five minutes' time.

Another factory worker is a mother of seven sons, proud-spirited, efficient, and accustomed to rule her family. The seven sons enlisted and she felt her claim to headship was endangered. She entered a munitions factory and, to soothe her pride, sent weekly to each son a detailed account of her industrial work. At length, the eldest son wrote that he thought his mother was probably killing more Germans than any of the family. Since then, she says, she has had peace of mind.

In another factory, in the West of England, there is an arduous munitions maker who works tirelessly through the longest shifts. Before her entry into the industrial world she was a stewardess on a passenger-ship. The vessel was torpedoed by a German submarine, and she was one of the few survivors. Daily she works off her hatred on a capstan lathe, hoping, as she tells the visitors, some day to get equal with the unspeakable Huns.

Then there is a typical case of a wife who has learned some of life's little ironies through her work on munitions production. Her husband, an old sailor, worked for the same firm before the war. He used to come home daily and complain of the hardness of his lot. It was 'a dog's life', he constantly reiterated, and his wife was careful to make reparation at home.

War broke out and the naval reserve man was recalled to sea. The firm were put to it, in the labour shortage, for a substitute, and invited the wife's aid. Having heard so much of the hardships of the work, she refused, but after some persuasion agreed to give the job a trial. At the end of a week, she surmised the task was not so hard as she contemplated; after a month had passed she realized the position. The job had been a capital excuse to ensure forgiveness for domestic short-comings. The wife awaits her husband's return with a certain grim humour.

Having arrived in the engineering trades, actuated by whatever motives, the woman munitions maker has more than justified the hopes of the pioneer employers who sponsored her cause. As soon as organized labour agreed that trade union rules and pre-war shop practice should be suspended for the duration of the war, women were rapidly initiated in the simple repetition processes of shell-making and shell-filling. Machinery was adapted to the new-comers, and the skilled men workers were distributed amongst the factories to undertake the jobs possible only to experienced hands.

DILUTION

Thus, the principle of dilution, as old as Plato's *Republic*, which as a theory was reintroduced to British students by Adam Smith, has widely come into practice through the urgency of the war. Women have been successfully introduced into a new group of occupations, men have been 'upgraded', so that many semi-skilled men have become skilled; and the skilled men have been allocated entirely to employment on skilled jobs.

Once introduced to the munitions shops, women soon mastered the repetition processes, such as 'turning', 'milling' and 'grinding', as well as the simpler operations connected with shell-filling. The keenest amongst them were then found fit for more 'advanced' work where accuracy, a nice judgment, and deftness of manipulation are essential. Such are the processes connected with tool and gauge-making, where the work must be finished to within the finest limits—a fraction of the width of a human hair; such are the requirements for the work of overlooking, or inspection of output; and such are the many processes of aeroplane manufacture and optical glass production, upon which women are being increasingly employed.

They are also undertaking operations dependent on physical strength, which in pre-war days would have been regarded as wholly unsuitable to female capacity. War necessity has, however, killed old-time prejudice and has proved how readily women adapt themselves to any task within their physical powers. One may, for example, today, (as at time of first publication), watch women in the shipyards of the North hard at work, chipping and cleaning the ships' decks, repairing hulls, or laying electric wire on board H.M. battleships. High up in the gantry cranes which move majestically across the vaulted factory roof, one may see women sitting aloft guiding the movement of the huge molten ingots; in the foundries, one may run across a woman smith; in the aeroplane factories, women welders work be-goggled at the anvils.

An engineering shop is now sometimes staffed almost entirely by women 'hands', and it is no uncommon sight to find in the centre of the shop women operators at work on the machines; at one end a group of women tool-setters, and at another women gaugers who test the products of this combined women's labour. In the packing-rooms the lustier types of women may be seen dispatching finished shells, and on the factory platforms gartered women in tunic suits push the loaded trolleys to waiting railway-trucks for conveyance to the front. One of the most surprising revelations of the war in this country has, indeed, been the capacity of women for engineering work, and to none has the discovery been more surprising and more exhilarating than to the women themselves.

HEROISM IN THE WORKSHOP

The work has, in fact, called for personal qualities usually thought to be abnormal in women. The women in the engineering shops have disproved any such surmise. Where occasion has demanded physical courage from the workers, the virtue has leaped forth from the average woman, as from the average man. Where circumstances call for grit and endurance, there has been no shirking in the factories by the majority of the operators of either sex. The heroism of the battlefields has frequently been equalled by the ordinary civilian in the factory, whether man or woman. Sometimes incidents of women's courage in the works have been reported in the press as matters for surprise. They are merely typical instances of the spirit that animates the general mass of the workers in Great Britain.

A few examples may be added in illustration. On a recent occasion, a woman lost the first finger and thumb of her left hand through the jamming of a piece of metal in a press. After an absence of six weeks, she returned to work and was soon getting an even greater output than before.

Another instance relates to a serious accident in an explosives factory, when several women were killed and many were injured. Within a few days a considerable number of the remaining female operators applied and were accepted for positions in the Danger Zone at another factory. Another incident is reported from some chemical works in the North. The key controlling a valve fell off and dropped into a pit below, rendering the woman in charge unable to control the steam. An accident seemed imminent and the woman, in spite of the likelihood of dangerous results to herself, got down to the pit, regained the key and averted disaster.

In a shipyard on the North-East coast, a woman of 23 years had been engaged for some time in electric-wiring a large battleship. One day, when working overhead, a drill came through from the deck, piercing her cotton cap and entering her head. She was attended to in the firm's First Aid room and sent home. To the surprise of everyone concerned, she returned to work at 6 a.m. on the following day, and laughingly remarked that she was quite satisfied that it was better to lose a little hair than her head.

In the trivial accidents which are, of course, of more frequent occurrence, the women display similar calmness and will stand unflinchingly while particles of grit, or metal, are removed from the eyes, or while small wounds—often due to their own carelessness—are dressed and bound. The endurance displayed during the early period of munitions production, when holidays were voluntarily abandoned and work continued through Sundays, and in many hours of overtime, was no less remarkable in the women than in the men. Action is continuously taken by the Ministry of Munitions to reduce the hours of overtime, to abolish Sunday labour, and to promote the well-being of the workers, but without the zeal and courage of the women munitions makers the valour of the soldiers at the Front would often be in vain.

As the Premier remarked in a recent speech: 'I do not know what would have happened to this land when the men had to go away fighting if the women had not come forward and done their share of the work. It would have been utterly impossible for us to have waged a successful war, had it not been for the skill and ardour, enthusiasm and industry, which the women of the country have thrown into the work of the war'.

CHAPTER 2

Training the Munition Worker

When, in answer to the demand for shells and more shells, factories were built, or adapted to the requirements of war, it was soon found that a supply of suitable labour must be ensured, if the maximum output was to be maintained. The existing practice of the engineering shops, by which a boy arrived by gradual steps, counted in years, from apprenticeship to the work of a skilled operator, was obviously impossible where an immediate demand for thousands of employees of varying efficiency had to be fulfilled. The needs of the navy and army further complicated the problem by the withdrawal of men of all degrees of skill from factory to battlefield.

The discovery of an untapped reservoir of labour in women's work, and the adaptation of a larger proportion of machines to a 'fool-proof' standard, certainly eased the situation, yet the problem remained of the immediate provision of workers able to undertake 'advanced', as well as simple work, in the engineering shops. Factory employers were from the outset alive to the situation, and at once adopted measures for the training of newcomers within their shops, but harassed as the managers were by the supreme need for output, it was hardly possible to develop extensive schemes for training within the factory gates. Hence, arose a movement throughout the United Kingdom among the governing bodies of many institutions of university rank, among local education authorities, and among various feminist groups, to make use of existing Technical Schools and Institutions for the training of recruits in engineering work.

The effort was at first mainly confined to the instruction of men in elementary machine work, and the London County Council may fairly claim to have acted as pioneer in this connexion. Yet, as early as August 1915, a group of women connected with the National Union of Women's Suffrage Societies (of which Mrs. Fawcett, widow of a former Postmaster-General, is the president) decided to finance a scheme for the training of women oxy-acetylene welders, converting for this purpose a small workshop run by a woman silversmith.

It was soon observed by the Ministry of Munitions that these sporadic efforts—sometimes successful beyond expectation, and sometimes failing for want of funds, or for lack of intimacy between training-ground and factory employer—must be co-ordinated, if they were to tackle successfully the growing task imposed by war conditions. The conception of a training section for factory workers within the Ministry of Munitions arose, took root. The section was established in the early autumn of 1915.

In the October of that year, authority to finance approved training schemes throughout the country was given to the new department. Some fifty colleges and schools, undertaking independent schemes, were then brought into touch with the ministry, and steps were taken to develop the existing systems. Equipment was thereby improved, recruiting of students stimulated, and a scheme for the payment of maintenance during training—such as the Manhattan Schools in New York had previously introduced to social investigators in this country—was established. The extension of the courses of training from instruction in simple processes to such advanced engineering work as lead-burning, tool-setting, and gauge-making soon followed, and was accompanied by necessary theoretical instruction in the methods of calculation of fine measurements.

THE QUINTESSENCE OF THE WORK

For these advanced classes, men alone were at first eligible as students, women being only instructed at the outset in elementary parts of the work. In the early days, the women were invited 'to do their bit', by learning how to bore, how to drill, how to plane, how to shape, and above all, how to work to size. The chief battle of the Training Centre with regard to the instruction of women was then, and still remains, the implanting of a feeling for exactitude in persons accustomed to measure ribbons or lace within a margin of a quarter of a yard or so, or to prepare food by a guess-work mixture of ingredients. I remember, at the beginning of a course of training for women, how an instructor at a large metropolitan centre remarked that 'ninety-nine *per cent.* of the new students do not know what accuracy means,' and he detailed how difficult it was to instil into their mind 'that quintessence of their work.'

Scientific methods of tuition, helped no doubt by women's proverbial patience, have, however, enabled the lesson to be learned after a few weeks' intensive training. The courses last but six to eight weeks and, at the conclusion of the carefully graduated tasks, it is not too much to say that the success of the women has been, in an overwhelming number of cases, surprising both to teachers and pupils.

I have before me a batch of letters from factory employers, written in the early period of the training schemes. They all bear testimony to the value of the outside instruction. One manager notes how the trained women from the schools were able 'to become producers almost at once;' another states that the drafting of the women students from school to factory has enabled the work of munitions to be carried on 'with greater expedition than would otherwise have been the case,' and yet another, with a scarcely concealed note of astonishment, relates that his students were able to be engaged at once on 'all kinds of machinery, capstan lathes, turning lathes, milling and wheel cutting machinery.'

This discovery of the employer, of the potentialities of women's work in the engineering trades, soon led to a development of the instruction of female students in the Training Centres; more advanced machine work was added to the curriculum, as well as tuition in aeroplane woodwork and construction, in core-making and moulding, in draughtsmanship and electrical work, in optical-instrument making, including the delicate and highly-skilled work of lens and prism making.

New Training Centres are constantly being opened in provincial areas, the instruction being adapted to the needs of local factories. There are now (December, 1917) over forty training schools for engineering work in Great Britain, as well as nine instructional factories and workshops, and the proportion of women to men trained in all the processes may be reckoned roughly as two to one.

The system of instruction is based, in some of the centres, on the general principle that the school undertakes the preliminary work of tuition in the simpler engineering processes; the instructional factory, or workshop, specializing in the more skilled processes, acts as a clearing-house for promising students from the schools. The urgency of warfare does not, however, permit the application of any hard-and-fast rules. I have seen specimens of some of the most 'advanced' work produced in a school; indeed, the delicate work of lens polishing and

17

centring, the intricacies of engineering draughtsmanship, the precise art of tool-setting and gauge-making have become specialisms of the schools in certain localities.

As I write, the face of an eager girl of 21 years recurs to memory. She was showing me, the other day, a master gauge produced at a school in the Eastern counties. 'I made it all myself,' she said joyfully, 'dead exact, and all the other gauges of this size in the school are made from it. I have just been appointed assistant instructor in gauge-making.' When it is recalled that the deviation in the measurements of a gauge is only tolerated within such limits as a $^{3/}10000$ part of an inch, the production in a school of a master gauge, 'dead exact' in all its dimensions, is a proof that the student has already gone some way in the mastery of the craft of the engineer.

THE INSTRUCTIONAL FACTORY

On the other hand, the instructional factory is often forced by war conditions to enrol raw recruits who seem likely material for the urgent needs of surrounding factories. In such cases, the candidate is placed on trial for a week or two in the instructional workshop, as in the school. If, at the close of the period of probation, she is deemed unsuitable, she is advised at that preliminary stage to return to her former occupation.

Speaking generally, the rejects are extraordinarily few, and although it would be premature to draw definite conclusions, the experience of the training section suggests that there is considerable latent capacity for engineering work in a large number of women. A tour of the instructional workshops emphasizes the point; everywhere, women may be seen mastering in the short intensive course the one advanced job for which each is being trained. In the instructional workshop, the atmosphere of a school is exchanged for that of a factory, the conditions of a modern engineering shop being reflected within its precincts. Thus the students 'clock on and off' on arrival and on departure, observe factory shifts, work on actual commercial jobs, obtain their tools from an attached store, and so on. The work varies in these Instructional factories as in the engineering shop of the commercial world.

In one section of such a hall of tuition you may see the women intent on the production of screws, or bolts, or nuts; in another part, such objects as fuse needles may be in the course of manufacture. You stop to see the magic which is answerable for the birth of the tiny factor which shall detonate the explosive, and you are amazed to find

TURNING THE COPPER BAND OF A 9.2-INCH HIGH-EXPLOSIVE SHELL

DRILLING SAFETY-PIN HOLE IN FUSE

INSPECTING AND GAUGING FUSES

TURNING THE OUTSIDE AND FORMING THE NOSE-END OF A 9.2-INCH
HIGH-EXPLOSIVE SHELL

that a fuse needle requires six tools for its production and eight to nine gauges for testing the accuracy of its measurements. Or, you may perhaps pause before a machine which is turning out tiny grub screws. To see a rod of steel offer itself, as it were, to the rightful instruments on a complicated machine to impress the thread and slit, to watch it proceeding on its way until a tiny section is divided and a complete screw is handed over to a tray outside the machine, is, to the uninitiated, a miracle in itself.

To see the whole of these complicated processes guided and operated by a smiling girl makes one hopeful for the national industries of the future. Setters-up of tools are at work in another section of the same instructional factory and at other machines are students grinding, milling, or profiling.

You may then visit another instructional factory to find that aircraft is the specialty. I recall one such training-ground in a bay of an aeroplane factory. There the girls learn almost every part of aircraft production, from the handling of the tiny hammers used on the woodwork for the body and wings, to the assembling, or putting together the tested parts. In this training factory, a system prevails of lectures by the practical instructors on the use of necessary tools; questions from the students are encouraged at the close of the lecture, and, I was informed, when on one occasion I was one of the audience, that the saving of the instructor's time by the adoption of this method was beyond expected results.

Again, you may visit an instructional factory where foundry work is included in the curriculum, or where advanced machine work is a feature. I have stood in one instructional workshop where some 600 machines were whirring simultaneously, and where the spirit of energy and goodwill of both students and instructors seemed as tangible as the metal objects produced. In this institution all the accomplished work is for production; night as well as day shifts are worked, and the needs of our armies, or those of our Allies, are frankly discussed with the operators. There is no occasion for other incentive: raw recruits, students from the schools, discharged soldiers from the front, men unfit for active service, all these denizens of the training-shop vie with each other to produce a maximum output.

It speaks volumes for this workshop that in spite of the continual changes of operators—each set of students remaining only for a course of six to eight weeks—it is entirely maintained on a commercial basis. To reach such a standard in these circumstances is to imply that the heroism of the workshop has become an ingrained habit in operators and staff.

First Steps in Industrial Life

I remember watching in this training-ground the manufacture of small aero-engine parts, exact in dimensions to within the smallest limits of tolerance. I put a query as to the wastage of material in such an operation, when handled by comparative newcomers. 'Scrapping from this process', replied the production manager with pride, 'does not exceed a total average of one *per cent*.' The women at work at the time had come from the most varied occupations. A large proportion had never worked outside their own home, others were domestic servants, cooks, housemaids, and so on, others were dressmakers from small towns, and one, I recall, was an assistant from a spa, where she had been engaged handing out 'waters' to invalids. 'It is not the rank of society from which the student is drawn that matters,' remarked an instructor; 'it is the personality of the individual that counts.'

Every care has been taken by the Ministry of Munitions to make it easy for women of all classes to participate in their schemes of instruction. The middle class girl who has never undertaken independent work, the woman who has always lived and worked within the shelter of her own home, undoubtedly felt in many cases debarred from entering industrial life. The necessity of living away from her family, in order to enter a training-school, the absence of home conditions in school or factory, the dread of an entirely masculine superintendence, all helped to strengthen artificial barriers between potential students and the needed engineering work. The training section, watching the development of its schemes, became aware of the necessity of making arrangements for students from the welfare point of view, and an organization has thus developed by which the first steps in industrial life are made easy for the most apprehensive of new-comers.

Girl students by rail are met by a responsible woman official and are accompanied to suitable lodgings, or to hostels. In the event of pressure in accommodation, the new student is introduced to temporary apartments, or to a 'Clearing Hostel', where she awaits in comfort a vacancy. In the large Training Centres, a woman supervisor is in charge. She makes all arrangements as to the provision of meals, rest-rooms, cloak-rooms, First-Aid centres, and so on, and is ready to advise the women students on all points relating to their personal interests.

Women students are also enabled to wear a khaki uniform, as members of the Mechanical Unit of the Women's Legion, a privilege found to be of distinct value to girls unaccustomed to steering an independent course in the more boisterous streams of life. The appreciation of the students of the safe-guarding of their individual desires crops out in unexpected places. In a handful of correspondence from students, one gleans such remarks as the following:

Mrs. H. never spares herself any trouble as long as she can make things pleasant for me, she considers it her "war work" to make munition workers happy, and it is very nice to meet people that appreciate what we are doing for our country.. . .

We were met at the station by the works motor. All at once we turned up an avenue of lime-trees and drew up at the door of our country estate. It is a real lovely house and we revel in the glories of fresh air, lawns and gardens, good beds and well-spread tables. We cross a field to the works. Dinner and tea await us when we get here, and there is a well-stocked vegetable garden to give us fresh vegetables, so we all feel indeed that our lines are fallen in pleasant places, and we are very grateful.

In these ways a bridge has been built by the Ministry of Munitions between the normal life of the women in this country and the work in the munitions factory.

CHAPTER 3

At Work—1

Arrived in the munitions factory, the newcomer, whether from a Government Training Centre, or from another occupation, is given two or three weeks' trial on the task she has come to undertake. Only a very small proportion of the women offering their services—one experienced manager puts it at 5 *per cent.*—are found unsuitable, and these are discharged during the probationary period.

Except in the case of those who have received a preliminary training, or of those who have merely transferred their energies from other factory work, the average woman has, at the initial stage in the munitions shops, to overcome an instinctive fear of the machine. Occasionally, the fear is intensified into an unreasoning phase of terror. 'One has to coax the women to stay with such as these,' said one understanding foreman, pointing to a monster machine with huge-toothed wheels. 'We don't ask a woman to sit alone with these at first, for she wouldn't do it, so we put a man with her, and let her sit and watch a bit, and after a while she loses her fear and won't work anything else, if she can help it.'

The women, in fact, soon get attached to the machines they are working, in a manner probably unknown to the men. 'I've been here a year on this machine, and I can't do near so well on any other,' is a remark many a girl has made to me as I have watched her on a difficult job. From time to time, a girl will even confess that she 'can't bear to think of someone on the night-shift working *her* machine'. An understanding has arisen between the machine and the operator which amounts almost to affection. I have often noticed the expression of this emotion in the workshops; the caressing touch of a woman's fingers, for instance, as a bore is being urged on to the job on the machine. This touch, which cannot be taught, or imparted, enables the operation to be started in the most effective method possible, and goes to the making of an excellent and accurate worker.

The femininity of the worker has, however, its drawbacks, and for the sake of successful handling of women in the munitions factory, it is as well that these psychological points should be noted. If, for example, a machine is out of gear, or if the operation is held up for any other cause, the women munition makers will sometimes behave in an unreasonable manner, quite bewildering to a foreman accustomed only to dealing with men. The temporary cessation of work may make only a slight money difference to the woman operator by the end of the week: 'not enough to fuss about,' as the foreman judges. But the woman nevertheless often *does* fuss, because in her eyes the wages do not loom so large as the interruption to her work. She 'hates standing-by', she will say, for she cannot express the emotion of which she is but dimly conscious, that a woman's deep instinct is to give freely of her fullness, and it frets her very soul to be balked in the middle of a job.

Other initial obstacles in the employment of 'new' female labour in the factories result from the exchange of the manifold duties of the woman in her own home for repetition work performed in the company of hundreds of other human beings. These difficulties are, however, soon overcome, and the newcomer, generally speaking, rapidly becomes one of a large and merry company. The whirr of the wheels and the persistent throb of the machinery may at first distract her, but after a short time the factory noises are unnoticed, save as an accompaniment to her thoughts, her laughter, or her song. I have indeed met in the England of today nothing more inspiriting, outside the soldiers' camps, than the women munition workers at work or at play.

In August 1916, there were some 500 different munitions processes upon which women were engaged. Today, (as at time of first publication), they are employed upon practically every operation in factory, in foundry, in laboratory, and chemical works, of which they are physically capable. Within the limits of this publication it is not possible to follow them into every field of their endeavours, yet a glance at their work in a few typical products may give some slight indication of women's contribution to Britain's effort in the World War.

SHELLS AND SHELL CASES

Of the numbers of operations that go to the making of a shell, women now undertake every process, in some works, including even the forging of the billets in the foundry. It was the urgent need of a

ASSEMBLING FUSES

COOLING SHELL FORGINGS

OPERATING A LUMSDEN PLAIN GRINDER
RE-FORMING 8-INCH HIGH-EXPLOSIVE CUTTERS

greatly increased output of shells in 1915 which led to the widespread introduction into the engineering shops of female labour, and the women have repaid this unique opportunity by their unqualified success. So rapid, and so marked, has been their progress in shell production that by the spring of 1917 the official announcement was justified, that, by March 31 of that year, government contracts for shells of certain dimensions would only be given where 80 *per cent.* of the employees were women.

At first, the women were mainly engaged in simple machine operations, such as boring, drilling, and turning, or in filling the shells. They are, at present, working hydraulic presses, guiding huge overhead cranes, 'tonging', or lifting the molten billets, 'setting', or fitting the tools in the machines, inspecting and gauging, painting the finished shell cases, making the boxes for dispatch of the finished product, and trucking these when finally screwed up and ready for exit from the factory to the Front. It is not possible to describe here in detail women's entire contribution to the production of a shell, but, from foundry to railway truck, she has become an alert and promising worker.

In the foundry, her appearance is as yet exceptional, yet in the North country it is no unusual sight to find a woman in the cage suspended from the overhead travelling crane, operating its protruding arm. Now, she will pick up with the clumsy iron fingers a pig of iron and thrust it into the glowing depths of a furnace, or she will lift the red-hot billet and bring it to the hydraulic press, where it is roughly hollowed into its predestined shape.

In the shell shop proper you may watch the woman operator on some scores of processes; at one machine, she may be attacking the centre of the billet with a revolving nose, at another she may be 'turning' the outside of a shell. The shavings curl off in this process like hot bacon rind and fall in iridescent rings around her: blue, purple, peacock, or gleaming silver. Or, you may watch the woman worker 'threading' the shell, a process by which the screw threads are provided, into which the nose of the shell is afterwards fitted; or, you may stand and marvel at the skill of the worker who so deftly rivets the base-plate into the shell's lower end. But, perhaps, the most attractive operation to the visitor to the shell shop is the fitting and grooving of the shell's copper band, a process which leaves the machine and worker half-hidden in the glory of sunset tints, as the copper scrap falls thickly from the machine.

At every stage, the shell is gauged and tested, examined and reexamined, since accuracy is the watch-word of its production. Sometimes, the machine-operator will gauge her own product; at other stages, the shell passes into the hands of women overlookers of the factory, the final tests being made by government 'viewers'. The inside, as well as the outside of the shell is submitted to such inspection, and you may see women peering into the interior of the shells, aided by the light from a tiny electric bulb, mounted on a stick. This contrivance is thrust successively into rows and rows of shells.

Women are now exclusively used for the painting of the shells, a process accomplished, not by means of a brush and paint-pot, but by the operator playing a fine electrically-worked syringe on to the surface of the shell. This process is undertaken in what is often called 'the butcher's shop,' the shells, in pairs, being swung up on a rope into a compartment where the operator works from behind a protective iron screen.

In the filling shops, women's devotion to their work has been proved once and again. Whether the process undertaken be in company of a few comrades, or in isolated huts where lonely vigils are kept over stores of explosives, the munition-girls are hardly known to flinch in their duty.

Sometimes, they have volunteered to work throughout the night when air-raids are in progress, at other times, women-workers have returned to the danger zone immediately after some bad experience there; and, in every case, the woman worker in the filling factory cheerfully sacrifices much which she holds dear in life. It may signify but little to a man to give up his small personal possessions whilst at work in the danger areas, but to many a woman worker it means much, that she may not wear a brooch, or a flower, while on duty, and that her wedding-ring, the only allowable trinket, must be bound with thread while she works. Her tresses, which she normally loves to braid, or twist into varying fashions, must also be left hairpinless beneath her cap. She must relinquish her personal belongings before going to her allotted task; no crochet-hook or knitting-pin may accompany her into the zone where friction of steel, or hard metal, might spell death to a multitude of employees. Yet this sacrifice of individuality is given freely by the woman in the filling shop, and she is still merry-hearted and blithe as she fills the small bags with deadly powder, or binds the charge which shall fire the shell.

When the shell is finally filled and passed 'O.K.,' or perfect, it is a woman who packs it into its box and who wheels it on a truck, sometimes for a mile or more over narrow platforms, to hand it to another woman who stacks it into the waiting railway-wagon. Anyone who has watched throughout the production of a shell in a factory of today can only echo a well-known author's recent salute: '*Hats off to the Women.*'

IN THE FUSE SHOP

The fuse, that small and complicated object which explodes the shell, is a war-product now largely produced by women's labour. A few inches in length, it requires some hundreds of operations for its manufacture, even if the initial processes on the metal are excluded from the count. In section, it looks like a complicated metal jig-saw puzzle of exquisite finish and cohesion: viewing it externally, a child might mistake it for a conjurer's 'property,' a bright metal egg, or roll often surrounded by a metal ring marked with time measurements.

The care and accuracy necessary for the production of this small object can hardly be imagined by the uninitiated: it is measured and remeasured in every diameter, since on its perfection depends the life of the gunner and his team. The fuse shop is usually characterized by its cleanliness and quietude. I recall one such shop stretching far away into distance both in length and breadth. Under its roof some 1,500 women were at work. Conversation could be held in any part of the shop, undisturbed by the usual factory noises. The fuse parts are, indeed, so small that the machinery is necessarily light, and in such a shop it is dexterity and accuracy that tell, rather than physical strength.

Rows of graceful women and girls were standing at their machines, and I recall how their overalls and caps of varied hues made a rainbow effect, as one watched from a distant corner. Some were in cream colour and some in russet-brown, or apple green, the caps sometimes matching the overall and sometimes offering a strong contrast. A splash of purple, or a deep magenta, mingled with the head-dresses of softer hue, for in this shop, away from the danger zone, no insistence was made on uniformity of factory costume. Other women, wearing a distinctive armlet, were passing in and out between the rows of workers, now stopping and bending over a machine, now making some bright remark to the operator, as a ripple of laughter indicated, or again, pointing out in sterner wise some danger, or some error in the job. These itinerary women are the overlookers, who since the war have perfected themselves in their special job and can now supervise the operators.

At long tables, other women were sitting; some quite elderly and grey-haired, some mere girls. They were measuring with small gauges parts of the fuse, some the size of a good-sized bead. There are 150 different gauges authorized for the measurement of one type of fuse, and in practice even more are used, to ensure perfection of accuracy. I stood spell-bound at one of these gauging tables and watched the examination of small screws and flash plugs. There were six little squares of felt on the table, on which the examiner placed rejects, classified according to the detected flaw. The work proceeded with the utmost dispatch, the 'accepted' or 'perfect' heap growing as if by magic.

At another table, a girl was testing springs of about an inch long. If any of these showed the smallest fraction too much length after being submitted to a given pressure, they were put aside as 'scrap'. At yet another table, tiny fuse needles were being examined for length, thickness of phlange, and accuracy of point, and on a high flat desk, near a machine, I noticed seventeen different gauges were ranged for the examination of the percussion end of the fuse-body, one ten-thousandth part of an inch being the limitation or variation allowed in such parts.

When all the parts have been examined they are passed to other tables for assembling, or putting together. In this operation almost superhuman care is required, and the work is reserved for the best operators and time-keepers as a reward for long service. 'Assembling' is regarded as the plum of the fuse-room. The operators are well aware of the importance of the task, as they stow away in the time fuses the pea-ball, pellet, spring, stirrup, ferrule, and other components of the fuse. The needle is fixed by blows from a small hammer, and at length the fuse is completed and passes out of the room of its creation to receive its 'filling' from other hands.

CARTRIDGES AND BULLETS

The production of cartridges and bullets is another branch of munitions production in which women are mainly employed. These objects, which, when completed, are together no longer than a ball-room pencil, make in their manufacture no great demand on physical strength.

On entering a cartridge and bullet shop, one is at once struck with its individuality. There is more stir and movement than in a fuse-room, but less of the imperiousness of the machinery than in the shell or gun shop. There is in the cartridge and bullet room still the whirr of wheels and, above that, the deep constant throb of the driving-force, that makes conversation almost inaudible to the newcomer. But beneath this bass accompaniment, one can hear the lesser sounds belonging to the cartridge and bullet-room alone. There may be the buzz of the circulating gas machines—which resemble miniature merry-go-rounds—the tap, tap, of the cartridges as they are thrown out of the machine into a box below, and the tinkle of bullets as they are poured into weighing machines, or on to tables, or into huge barrels, such as are used on the wharves for the transport of herrings.

A cartridge and bullet-shop sometimes is as animated and as picturesque as an open-air market under a southern sky. I remember such a shop where the girls were in various factory costumes, some at the machines in khaki and some in cream-coloured overalls and caps; some, who were 'trucking', or removing the product in boxes, were in cream trouser-suits, with smart head-dresses fashioned from brightly-coloured oriental handkerchiefs. In between the rows of girls men in dark suits were passing to and fro, now stopping to examine, or alter a machine and now taking up a box of bullets and pouring out its glittering contents like a silver stream, so that the output from each worker might be weighed and assessed.

Through an open door, at one side of the shop, one could see other men, like stern magicians, dropping cartridges into vats of acid, and just to the side of the vats I caught sight of two girls vigorously shaking a sack of cartridges, hot from the furnace. As they shook, they sang an army refrain: 'Take me back to dear old Blighty,' with a chorus of laughter. At the extreme end of the shop, near the door whence the product made its exit, were long narrow tables, piled with bullets, reminding one of a haul of silver sprats on the quayside. These were the inspecting tables where the bullets receive minute attention from women viewers.

The women's work in the bullet-shop is of extraordinary interest to the onlooker, although many of the processes must be infinitely more monotonous, from the worker's standpoint, than operations in other munitions productions. The elongation of the little metal vessel, resembling an acorn-cup, into a full-length cartridge, or bullet, necessitates many operations in which the dexterity of human fingers and the ingenuity of the machine both come into play. In the shop I recall, in one machine employed for semi-annealing, the cartridge was being 'fed' into a metal revolving plate. This passed behind an asbestos screen into a double row of gas jets, where the semi-annealing or hardening process was being accomplished. The dexterity of the operators was so great that one woman was often feeding two machines, apparently without effort, and never missed placing the cartridge into the correct aperture in the revolving plate.

In another process, I watched young girls sitting round a table and placing bullets into circular apertures in small trays, resembling solitaire-boards. Many of the girls were working with such speed that it was impossible to follow the movements of their fingers, but they, unconscious of their prowess, worked with averted heads, smiling in amusement at the visitor's astonishment.

In yet another operation, it was the machine that held one's attention. The operator was feeding cartridges into a metal band which slipped out of view while the process of 'tapering' was performed. When finished, a metal thumb and index finger appeared, which delicately picked up the cartridges, one by one, and threw them aside. The displaced cartridge then hopped out of the machine into a box at the side of the machine.

Entranced by the many mysteries in the production of cartridges and bullets in the shop I am recalling, I had not noticed that the tea-interval had arrived, and suddenly found that the work-room was almost empty of human beings. Only two girls remained. They were sitting sewing, whilst they devoured thick slices of bread and butter out of a newspaper packet. The woman inspector, who was my guide, turned sharply. 'What are you doing here?' she said, 'Eating your tea in the workshop, instead of outside, or in the canteen. Be off at once into the fresh air.' Then, with the indignation fading out of a good-humoured face: 'What next?' she said.

Looking out of the open door at the streams of bright and happy girls laughing, singing, dancing, and running, as only healthy youth can do in the midst of these dark days of war, I seemed to see other and brighter days ahead stretching out into the years of the future, when the workfolk would all taste a fuller joy in life. With renewed hope, I gave her back her challenge: 'Well! and what next?'

CHAPTER 4

At Work—2

THE MAKING OF AIRCRAFT

The production of aircraft, undertaken in this country on a large scale only since the outbreak of the war, has fallen more naturally into the hands of women. The work is for the most part light, and the new factories, often erected in open country, are bright, airy, and largely free from the noise of machinery. Added to these special attractions to the woman worker, there is apparently a distinct appeal to the youth of both sexes and to women of all ages in anything connected with the art of flying.

It is no secret that our output of aircraft is steadily increasing, and that during 1917 it has been doubled. In one factory in London, the output has been trebled within three months; in Lancashire, there are instances in which it has been doubled, and other areas show an improved production varying from 25 to 50 *per cent*. Yet the increased demand for labour for this work has always been immediately answered, and there is a steady flow into the factories of the best type of women workers from every class of society. Here and there, one already meets a woman who, during the short period of the war, has risen to be manager or partner in an aircraft factory. Unconsciously, such a one emphasizes the fact that the mastery of the element of the future is likely to be an affair of both the sexes.

A visit to any aeroplane factory repeats the hint, and reveals the extraordinary versatility of skill latent in women, which can well be applied to this form of industry. 'Women *must* have been cabin'd, cribbed, and confined before the war', said a foreman in taking me over his shop in an aircraft works. 'Look what they can do at this kind of job, and yet many of them are ladies, from homes where they sat

ENGRAVING METAL PARTS FOR COMPASSES

COLOURING AEROPLANE PLANES

CHIPPING AND GRINDING BLADES OF CAST IRON PROPELLER
WITH PORTABLE TOOLS

WOMAN ACTING AS MATE TO JOINER. MAKING SEA-PLANE FLOATS

about and were waited upon.' The wonder of it cannot fail to impress a visitor, since only four years ago women were allowed to undertake in aircraft construction merely those parts which convention deemed suitable for feminine fingers: such processes, for instance, as the sewing of the wings by hand, or by machine, or the painting of the wood-work.

Today, they undertake almost every other process both at the carpenter's bench and in the engineering shop, and the chief impression you carry away from a stroll through such a factory is that the women are thoroughly at home in the work. The operations are often so clean that the workers' overalls and caps of the daintiest shades of pink, blue, white, and heliotrope, remain fresh; the material for aeroplane parts is usually so light that the handling of it presents no difficulty to a slip of a girl. When within the works, the visitor is constantly stimulated to the thought that the hand which rocks the cradle should obviously be the one to make the air-machine.

One expects, of course, women's familiarity with the occupation in the room where the fine Irish linen is cut out and fashioned into wings. One is not surprised at the facility with which the measuring and cutting out are accomplished, and, maybe, an emotion of admiration arises, similar to that evoked by the contemplation of old tapestries, when one watches the hand-sewing of a seam in a wing of some 10 feet in length. Not a stitch of the button-holing of such a seam deviates by a hairbreadth from its fellows. Such work has, however, been women's province through the ages.

But a new sensation is awakened in the carpenter's shop where women are working with dexterity at the bench, handling woodwork like the men, now dealing with delicate wooden ribs, or again, fashioning propellers out of mahogany or walnut with such nicety that there is not the slightest deviation between the dimensions of a pair. In the room where the linen is stretched over the wooden ribs, I have seen women working with tiny hammers, giving fairy blows that never miss their mark on tiny nails.

It is with fascination that a visitor stands by be-goggled women as they undertake the welding of metal joints by the oxy-acetylene process. Here, conscientiousness is a vital quality in the operator, since an undetected flaw in the weld, as a works foreman recently remarked, 'might easily send an airman to Kingdom Come'. For this process, women of education are more often selected.

It is with awe that you watch the women at work on the metal parts of the aeroplane, drilling, grinding, boring, milling on the machine, or soldering tiny aluminum parts for the fuselage, and in each process gauging and re-gauging, measuring and re-measuring. Women also work on aero-engines, and help in the manufacture of the magneto, the very heart of the machine. They even undertake special processes, which before the war were only entrusted to a select body of men. I stood one day, for example, watching a woman splicing steel rope, a process]undertaken in pre-war days by sailors. She was working with extraordinary speed and unconcern, and had learned the job in three or four days. Before then, she told me, she had been her employer's cook.

But the most alluring scene of all is the assembling of aircraft. The infinite number of separate parts are now ready; they have been tested by factory overlookers and retested by government inspectors. The greatest care is taken in these examinations: it is the only possible insurance of the lives of the brave youths on their journey above the clouds. All the workers know this, and the seriousness of the job is reflected on their faces. But now all the parts are ready and to hand in the erecting shop. Then wings and propeller are added to body, the engine and leather-upholstered seats introduced, the electric apparatus fitted up, the compass, ammunition box and other instruments and weapons placed in position.

The aeroplane is at length complete, and stands in the hangar like some great bird, with outstretched pinions, awaiting its first flight into the Unknown. Women undertake every process of this assembling, and have acquired familiarity with all the parts. This was put to the test recently in a certain works when a woman operator was directed to dismantle a machine. Without hesitation, she stripped the complex network of the structural stay-wires and the control wires, and then re-assembled them, correct in every particular, at the first attempt.

Optical Instruments

Of the many industries developed by the war, the production of optical instruments offers a striking example of rapid progress. Before 1914, the optical glass industry of Europe was largely in the hands of Germany and Austria, and the outbreak of hostilities meant the total closing of that market to the Allies. The lack of optical instruments thus occasioned was at first a source of grave national peril, since optical glass provides, as it were, eyes for both navy and army. The eyes of the guns are the range-finder, the director, the sighting telescope, periscope, prism binoculars, and other instruments for observing fire and correcting the aim; the tank would be blind without its periscope, and observations are made from aircraft by means of photographic cameras and lenses.

At sea, the tale is repeated; the submarine requires at least one eye, and the submarine chaser needs many, while, by means of optical instruments, the naval gunner can fire at a target which is about 15 to 20 miles away. The very health of the army depends, in great measure, on optical glass, since the Royal Army Medical Corps fights malaria and other diseases due to parasites, which must be magnified by a microscope a thousand times before they can be identified. Hence, the solution of the problem of optical munitions was a vital matter in the early days of the war.

With characteristic energy, Great Britain set to work and soon restored a languishing trade. The task was enormous; the industry had to be revived from its very foundations. The production of the peculiar types of glass required for optical instruments in itself presented a formidable obstacle, even its principal ingredient, a special quality of sand, being formerly derived mainly from Fontainebleau and Belgium. But by widespread investigation efficient substitutes were soon discovered, the problem of mixing the ingredients was at length solved, formulæ for special glasses devised, and we are now producing large quantities of optical glass of perfect quality. The production of the raw material was, however, only a first step in obtaining an adequate supply of optical instruments.

Numbers of delicate processes stand between the rough glass and the finished implement. The glass must be cut, ground, and curved exactly to the requisite design, which in itself takes many days of high mathematical computation; it must be smoothed and polished, cleaned with meticulous care, and adjusted to a nicety in the particular instrument for which it is fashioned. The difficulties and pitfalls are incalculable; from start to finish the glass obeys no fixed laws, but answers only to the skilled handling of the scientist and craftsman. 'Optical glass is the mule of materials,' comments a recent writer with sincerity.

The absence of requisite labour for what was practically a new industry was a serious menace, and it is to the credit of Englishwomen that, as soon as the need for their services in this direction was made known, they stepped without hesitation into this unfamiliar and highly skilled industry. Their success therein is remarkable, and many, from such callings as high-class domestic service, kindergarten instruction, music teaching, blouse and dressmaking, have achieved a wonderful record in the delicate and highly technical processes of lens-smoothing and polishing and in the production of prisms of faultless polish and cut.

There is, I take it, no more interesting munitions development than in factories where these lenses and prisms are produced. The work is so fine and so delicate that one feels it might be more suitably transferred for manipulation to elves, or fairy folk, who might undertake the various processes standing at a large-sized toad-stool. But with the stern reality of war upon us, willing feminine fingers have had to be trained to handle these lenses, the smallest of which, when ranged in trays, resemble a collection of dewdrops, and the largest of which would easily fill the port-hole of an ocean-liner.

Optical glass when it comes into the workshop has the appearance of small blocks of rough ice of a greyish hue. These blocks are roughly sliced and cut into shape by a rotating metal disk charged with diamond dust. The prisms and lenses in their initial stage are then handed on to women, who complete the work on their surfaces. Each process has its particular lure for the interested visitor. You may watch the slices of glass being shaped into prisms by handwork against the tool; you may follow these embryo prisms through the various processes of smoothing and polishing until a small magnifying prism is obtained for use in a magnetic compass, or until a large prism is completed suitable for a submarine periscope. You may follow the creation of a lens from the roughing and grinding of the glass slices with emery, or carborundum, until the approximate shape is given, or you may follow a later process of sticking the smaller lenses on to pitch, so that they may form a single surface for smoothing and polishing.

Again, you may watch the superlatively difficult operation of centring a lens. This task is necessary to ensure the polished surfaces of the lens running perfectly true and it requires a skilled touch and a trained eye to undertake it satisfactorily.

In a shop in a certain optical munitions factory I met the first woman who worked a centring machine in that area. She was formerly a housemaid, and told me that, at first, all the men had discouraged her from the job and had said it was 'impossible for a woman to do such work'. But she 'stuck it'—so she said—and in a few weeks, to her own surprise and the men's dismay, this peculiarly skilled job became familiar to her. 'Now I feel I am doing something,' she said in triumph. This sentiment was echoed by another worker in that factory who was accomplishing the surprising task of 'chamfering', or putting a tiny bevel onto the edge of a lens.

The large lenses measure only 2 inches in diameter; the smaller ones are about the size of a threepenny bit, and every operation, whether grinding, trueing, smoothing, polishing, or centring, must be accomplished with the utmost care. Even the final process in the manufacture of the lens or prism, 'wiping off', is fraught with responsibility to the operator. 'Wiping off,' or cleaning the lens, can only be done with a silken duster, for the finished glass, like a dainty lady, will tolerate the touch of nothing coarse.

In cases where the glass is graticulated, or marked with fine lines for measurement purposes, the task of 'wiping off' is of extraordinary difficulty; in the opinion of at least one foreman with whom I have discussed this question, the operation is only perfectly successful when performed by a girl's fingers. It is of supreme importance that no speck of dirt or hint of grease from a finger-mark be left on the glass when finally adjusted, or the instrument would become a source of danger to the user. No wonder that the feeling of the optical instrument workshop expresses itself in the words: 'Cleanliness is more than godliness at this job.'

The completed glass at length reaches the stage where it is set in its instrument, be it periscope, dial-sight, telescope, and so on. Although the most exact measurements have been observed both in the metal part and on the glass, small adjustments are necessary; for the fit must be so perfect that even if the metal case suffers shell-shock, the glass must still not rattle. But it is the metal alone which is submitted to alteration, and it is wonderful how women have been able to obtain sufficient dexterity to make these infinitesimal changes in the metal parts. One can see a mere girl undertaking such a task by giving the metal three or four delicate strokes from a file so fine that it would not hurt a baby's skin. Meantime, the lens or prism is finally examined (also by women) for size, scratches, and other imperfections, and is then recleaned. Girls and women take a full share in the production of the metal parts for the optical instruments and also assemble, or collect the parts, for the adjustment of the glass, but so far they do not generally adjust or test the completed instrument.

The operations used in the production of optical instruments for war purposes are, of course, similar to those required in the manufacture of implements used in peace-time, such as opera-glasses, telescopes, microscopes, surveying instruments, photographic and cinematograph apparatus, &c., and it is expected that women who have entered the new war-time industry will happily find themselves, when peace dawns, in possession of a permanent means of livelihood in a skilled occupation.

IN THE SHIPYARDS

'Ships, ships, and still ships': such is the main need of the Allies in this, the fourth year of the war. To answer this demand, every dockyard in the country is working at the highest pressure. Into this work, strange as it may seem to those familiar with the rough-and-tumble life of a shipyard, women have penetrated and have so far surmounted all obstacles in the tasks to which they have been allocated.

At first, dilution in shipyards was looked upon as a hazardous experiment. The work is mostly heavy and clumsy, and the type of men undertaking it, splendid fellows enough in their physique and general outlook, are mainly accustomed to dealings with the boisterous elements and with men comrades of their own pattern. Their attitude towards women, it was feared, would make for trouble immediately that the other sex was introduced as fellow-workers. Even the most optimistic amongst shipbuilders were aghast at the idea of women working shoulder to shoulder with men on board ship. Yet here and there a pioneer employer has arisen, and the experiment has been tried. It is succeeding unquestionably.

I have been into the shipyards and seen the amazing sight and am convinced of its expediency, at all events as a war-time measure. Special care must, of course, be taken in the planning and the supervision of women's work on board ship, but given the right type of inspectress, charge hand, and workers, there is no reason why women should not, in increasing numbers, fill the gaps in the shipyards, as in the factories. The women chosen to undertake such tasks are well aware of the service they are rendering to the nation at this juncture, and to the women workers the first day on board ship is one of supreme happiness. 'They are so excited when they actually get on board,' said a dockyard inspectress to me recently 'that they forget all about the difficulties and objections to the work.' It is well that this is so, for it is not too easy for the novice to move about below, even on a big battleship.

I was taken over one where the women were working. It was in a big yard crammed with shipping of every kind—so full that one could echo the words of the old Elizabethan, who said of a crowd: '*There was not room for a snail to put out its horns.*' A stiff breeze was blowing, and the sea beyond ran full and blue. The great battleship along the dock lay serene and stately, bearing, as it were, with grim humour the meddlesome tappings and chippings of impertinent human beings, who presumed to furbish her up. There were men on the conning-tower, busy with paint-pots, and there was a tangle of ropes and pots on the upper decks where the guns were biding their time. Men were calling lustily to each other, and were darting here and there as brisk and wholesome as the breeze.

'We go down here,' said the inspectress, pointing to a ladder as steep as the side of a house. She bounded down with the ease of an antelope. Another ladder, and yet another. The inspectress seemed to have forgotten their steep incline and I was left, a helpless landlubber, cautiously descending step by step. When I joined her in the engine-room she was already deep in conversation with one of her staff. And then I noticed the secret aid to her agility. All the women aboard ship were dressed in trouser suits. The suits, of blue drill for the supervisors, and of a similar material in brown for the labourers, were made with a short tunic, and the trousers were buckled securely at the ankle. A tight-fitting cap to match completed the smart workmanlike costume which permits of perfect freedom of movement in confined places. Without such a costume it would be hardly possible for women to work on board.

The women workers on this particular battleship were engaged in renewing electric wires and fittings, a job which requires a good deal of care and accuracy. On the lower deck, they were fitting up new cables and were perched in high places, here 'sweating in' a distribution box, there marking off the position for the wires. Others were drilling holes, others again were 'tapping', or making a thread in the holes. In the engine-room the women were busy stripping worn-out electric wiring and were working by the light of tall candles, as merry as a party preparing a Christmas tree.

Everywhere the women were working in pairs, an arrangement found especially advisable on board. Behind a small iron door we found one couple working on a fire-control in a nook where the entrance of a single visitor caused bad overcrowding. 'These are my mice', said the inspectress; 'they always get away into the cupboard-jobs, and very well they work there too. But we have to maintain a strict discipline on board, far stricter than anything known in the factories.'

No talking, I was informed, is allowed in that dockyard, during the working hours on board, between the sailors or men labourers and the women and there is constant supervision of the women employed. These work on board in parties of 20-22, each party being under the care of a charge hand. When the staff included three charge hands for supervision on board, an inspectress was appointed for this special branch of the work. The system seems to work well, and I noticed how the men and women had evidently accepted each other as comrades. Coming into a secluded gangway a man-labourer, who had finished his job, was unconcernedly shaving before a square of mirror, while two or three women just beyond went on, just as unconcernedly, tap, tapping at the electric fittings. There was no chaffing, no 'larking', between the men and women, but a sense of comradeship, such as one notices in a Co-education School.

The women on electric-wiring receive, in that dockyard, one month's instruction on dummy bulk-heads before going on board; their instructors—expert men—accompany them to the number of two to every party of twenty or so, and remain with them for ten to twelve months. After that, the women are able to work without an instructor, and I was an eyewitness to this arrangement on a cargo vessel, where electric wiring was also being undertaken.

Besides the work on board, women in dockyards are employed in the various engineering shops where almost every description of construction and repair work for vessels is undertaken. I have seen numbers of women at work in such an electrical department, winding armatures, making parts for firing-gear, polishing, or buffing and repairing electrical apparatus, &c. The work in such a repair section is full of interest and variety. From day to day the operators receive consignments of electrical apparatus damaged on board by the elements, or worse. Great dispatch is needed, and the women work with the utmost zeal and efficiency. I noticed them undertaking such varying operations as lackering guards for lamps and radiator fronts, repairing junction and section boxes, fire-control instruments, automatic searchlights, &c., and they were turning out their work, the foreman said, just like men. In the constructional department, women are now employed in making bulkhead pieces, or metal-work of various kinds, in oxy-acetylene welding, and occasionally in the foundry.

When it is recollected that before the war only elderly women—the grandmothers—were, generally speaking, employed in the dockyards, and those only on such ornamental tasks as flag-making or upholstery for yachts, it is hardly credible that the granddaughters are now working successfully on intricate processes and even at jobs where physical strength is a qualification.

'We can hardly believe our eyes,' said a foreman recently, 'when we see the heavy stuff brought to and from the shops in motor lorries driven by girls. Before the war it was all carted by horses and men. The girls do the job all right though, and the only thing they ever complain about is that their toes get cold.'

'They don't now', said a strapping young woman-driver, overhearing the conversation. 'We've got hot-water tins.' Then, in a low voice, for my ears alone, 'I love my work, it's ever so interesting.'

It is this note that one finds above all, amongst the women in the dockyards. The spirit of the sea, the almost forgotten heritage of an island population, has been stirred once more, and the sight of the good ships in harbour thrills the woman-worker, as the man, with a sense of independence, freedom, and love for '*this England, . . . this precious stone set in the silver sea*'.

No wonder that Englishwomen find their work in the dockyards 'ever so interesting'.

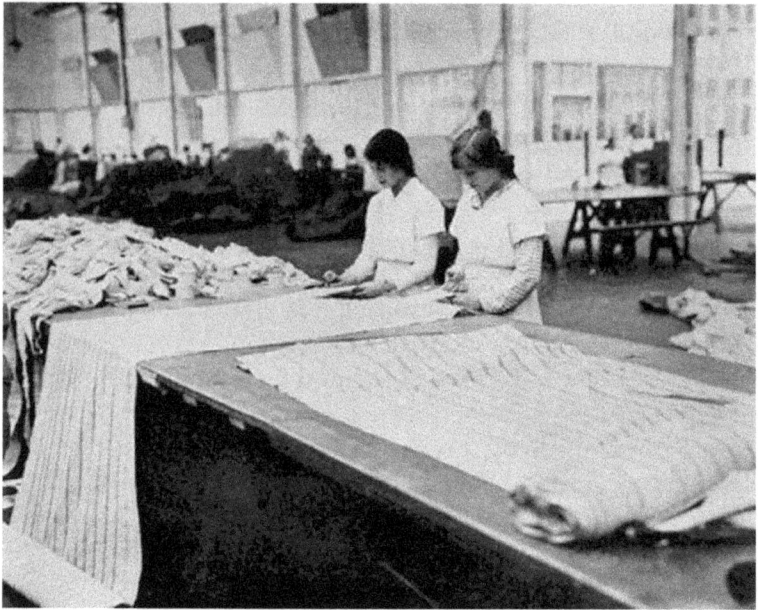

CUTTING FRAYED-EDGED TAPE

BRAZING TURBINE ROTOR SEGMENT

MOUNTING CARDS FOR DRY COMPASSES

TREADLE POLISHING-MACHINES, FOR SMOOTHING LENSES

CHAPTER 5

Comfort and Safety

The problems arising from the sudden employment of thousands of women in the factories have obviously been connected not only with the technical training of the workers and with the adaptation of machinery to their physical strength. Something had to be done, and that without delay, to ensure the comfort and safety in the workshops of these newcomers to industrial life.

In the first great rush for an increased munitions supply, war emergency dictated the temporary suppression of the Factory Acts. There was no demur within the factory gates. Women worked without hesitation from twelve to fourteen hours a day, or a night, for seven days a week, and with the voluntary sacrifice of public holidays. Their home conditions in a vast number of cases offered no drop of consolation. Many of these women were immigrants from remote corners of the Empire, or from faraway towns and villages of the United Kingdom. Housing accommodation in crowded industrial areas, or in a thinly populated countryside, was strained to breaking-point. Undaunted, these workers—many of whom had previously led an entirely sheltered life—rose before dawn to travel long distances to the factory, and returned to take alternative possession with a night-shift worker of a part share of a bedroom. The shameful conditions to which the factory children were subjected at the period of the Industrial Revolution seemed about to return.

WELFARE SUPERVISION

Such a state of things could not be tolerated, and Mr. Lloyd George, then Minister of Munitions, grasped the situation. He said:

'The workers of today are the mothers of tomorrow. In a war of workshops the women of Britain were needed to save Britain; it was

48

for Britain to protect them.'

Measures were immediately adopted to improve the conditions of the workers in the factory. A Departmental Committee was appointed to consider all questions relating to the health of munition workers, and at the Ministry of Munitions, on their recommendation, a Welfare and Health Department was established, charged with 'securing a high standard of conditions for all workers in munitions factories and more especially for the women and juvenile employees'. Since then, step by step the machinery is being set in motion for improving the conditions of life of munition workers.

Yet welfare work in the factory is no new thing in England. In pre-war days it had not, it is true, reached as widespread a development as in the United States, but as long ago as 1792 it was in practice in this country under another name. It is recorded of that period of one David Dale, whose factory was a model to his contemporaries, that he 'gave his money by shovelfuls to his employees' to find that 'God shovelled it back again.' From the early part of the nineteenth century, sporadic attempts were successfully made to improve the conditions of the factory workers over and above the requirements of legislation, and before 1914 a number of enlightened factory owners had won renown by the practice of welfare work within their precincts. The seal of official sanction has, however, only been gained since the war, through the influx of women into munitions trades.[1]

The Health of Munitions Workers Committee has, since its inception, investigated at factory after factory such questions as the employment of women, hours of labour, Sunday labour, juvenile employment, industrial fatigue, canteen equipment, the dietary of workers. It has published its conclusions in memoranda, stripped bare of officialism, so as to reveal with frankness facts acquired by scientists in touch with reality.

Working in connexion with this committee is the Welfare and Health Department of the Ministry of Munitions. It follows closely the suggestions of the experts, its Welfare officers moving up and down the country, now offering a suggestion to the management of a factory, and again, assimilating some practical experiment in welfare work, originated by a progressive factory-directorate. Thus, a pooling of ideas is being effected, and isolated experiments of value are now

---

1. Welfare work has since been officially extended to factories other than those engaged in munitions production by Clause 7 of the Police, Factories, &c. (Miscellaneous Provisions) Act (1916).

being propagated throughout the country.

But possibly one of the most valuable tasks of the Welfare and Health Department is the selection and training of candidates for the work of Welfare Supervision in the factories. A panel of approved candidates is kept in readiness, so that a busy factory-manager may have at hand a choice of welfare workers who will, if necessary, undertake the entire supervision of the personal interests of his female, or juvenile staff. These officers, after engagement by the factory management, are responsible solely to the firms that employ them and not to the Ministry of Munitions. In establishments where T.N.T. (Tri-nitro-toluene) is handled, the presence of a lady welfare supervisor is compulsory; in all national factories such an officer is recognized as a necessary part of the staff; and in controlled establishments, where a number of female operators are employed, the management is officially encouraged to make such an appointment.

In many cases, engineering shops are for the first time employing female operators, and the management depute with relief all questions as to the personal requirements of the 'new labour' to the lady superintendent; in other instances, such matters as the engagement of the employees, canteen arrangements, and so on, are placed in the hands of other officials. Hence, the duties of the lady welfare supervisor differ from factory to factory. Generally speaking, the supervisor, or lady superintendent within the factory is made responsible for some, or all, of the following matters:

1. She aids, or is entirely responsible for, the selection of women, girls, and boys for employment.

2. The general behaviour of the women and girls inside the factory falls under her purview.

3. The transfer of a woman employee from one process to another is suggested by the welfare Supervisor where health considerations make such an alteration advisable.

4. She is consulted on general grounds with regard to the dismissal of women and girls.

5. Factory conditions come under her observation, and reports are made, when necessary, to the management, on the cleanliness, ventilation, or warmth of the establishment.

6. The necessity of the provision of seats is suggested, where this is possible.

7. In large factories, where the canteen is under separate management, the welfare supervisor reports as to whether the necessary facilities are available for the women employees. In smaller factories, the welfare supervisor may be called upon to manage the canteen.

8. While not responsible, except in small factories, for actual attention to accidents, the welfare supervisor works in close touch with the factory doctors and nurses. She also helps in the selection of the nurses, and should see that their work is carried out promptly. She supervises the keeping of all records of accidents and illness in the ambulance room, and of all maternity cases noted in the factory. She keeps in touch with all cases of serious accident or illness and with the Compensation Department inside the works.

9. She supervises cloakrooms and selects the staff of attendants necessary for these.

10. The protective clothing supplied to the women at work comes under her supervision.

In large establishments where the female and juvenile staff is counted by the thousand, these multifarious duties are necessarily divided among many individuals, and the welfare work within the factory (Intra-mural Welfare, as it is now termed) develops into a department. A typical example of such an evolution may be seen at the Royal Arsenal, Woolwich. In pre-war days, the female staff numbered 125; today, (as at time of first publication), some 25,000 women are there at work.

The welfare supervision is happily in charge of a super-woman. In addition to her manifold duties she has trained a staff of assistants who, like herself, spare no effort to promote the health and happiness of those under their care. I have stood many an hour in this super-woman's office and watched her, surrounded by a throng of workers, fitting newcomers into vacancies, listening to reasons from others for a desired transference, or advising as to work, or meals, health, or recreation. No girl was refused a hearing, however trivial the difficulty, and a grievance as to the colour of a factory cap was discussed with as much attention with one employee as the causes of a 'shop' disagreement was with another complainant. I have accompanied her on visits through the works (the entire tour would take almost a week to accomplish), and have noted the diplomacy with which a suggested improvement in ventilation, or a needed cloak-room alteration, was discussed with the official in charge, and carried through. I have seen the faces of rows of workers light up as this modern Florence Nightingale passed through their shop, and have walked through the danger zone amazed at the arrangements for the protection of the worker.

What is true of the life in such large concerns as Woolwich Arsenal, or His Majesty's Factory, Gretna, is typical on a large scale of the development of welfare work in many a munitions factory throughout the kingdom. Protective clothing has been universally adopted, ambulance-rooms and rest-rooms have been opened, cloakroom accommodation improved, canteens established, sane recreation encouraged, and the protection of a women-police service introduced. In short, an atmosphere is being introduced by which the old-time barrier between employer and employed is being helped to disappear.

PROTECTIVE CLOTHING

So much has been accomplished since the advent of women in the munitions factories with regard to protective clothing for the worker that the subject might well fill a chapter to itself. A separate department in the Ministry of Munitions now concerns itself solely with its supply, and is continually experimenting with improvements in aprons, gloves, boots, caps, and tunics. Cotton overalls are now generally worn by the women employees and much thought has been given to the production of these garments in suitable materials and design. They are made with firmly stitched belts and with inset pockets, so as to avert accidents by contact of loose ends in the machinery, and are more often in the popular shades of khaki, or brown, with scarlet facings, or dark blue faced with crimson. But there is no set rule either as to colour, or design, so long as the principle of protection is followed.

Caps, which at first were much disliked by the workers, have at length found general favour, not, it is true, by reason of the immunity they offer against accident, but because they have been fashioned so as to add 'chic' to the wearer. They are usually of the 'Mob,' or 'Dutch' variety, and match the overall in colour and texture; they are all designed so that there is no pressure round the head. Sometimes, the cap of safety has been skilfully used as a mark of distinction, and one may see, in a shop staffed by women, the operators at the machines in khaki headgear, the setters-up of machines in scarlet caps, and the overlookers or inspectors of the product in bright blue head-dress.

For wet and dusty work there are trouser suits in cotton, woollen, or mackintosh, or tunic suits with knee breeches and leggings, or gaiters. Mackintosh coats are also provided for outdoor work in shipyards, or for trucking and lorrying, or for overhead crane-work within the factory.

Acid-proof and oil-proof aprons are now furnished for certain operations, and for other processes specially prepared gloves are supplied. The varieties in workshop gloves are now very great; they are made in such materials as India-rubber, canvas, or leather, or a union of these three, or in teon-faced canvas or teon-faced leather. Some are cuffless; others, for work in acids, have turned-up cuffs, and others again are gauntlets reaching the elbow. In every case, the process for which they are provided is minutely studied, and the fashion adopted is dictated by utility.

Footgear has also received a considerable amount of attention, and there are now available wellington boots, or half-wellingtons, for outdoor work, or wooden clogs for processes in the shops where the flooring is apt to become persistently wet.

But, possibly, factory fashions receive most care when designed for wearers in Filling shops. For these, suits in wool lasting-cloth are found satisfactory, the most popular and smartest being in cream-colour, faced with scarlet. Fire-proofed blue serge overalls and asbestos coats with caps of the same material are also employed in certain of these factories. For work in the danger zone no metal fasteners are permissible, and the coat, or overall, is cut so as to protect the neck and throat from contact with the powder used in the process.

Boots and shoes for this type of work are also specially designed. No iron must enter into their composition, the soles being either machine-sewn, or riveted with brass. Sometimes, cloth and India-rubber over-shoes are the chosen footwear of the danger zone, and in this case the fasteners must also be free from iron. These precautions are no mere fad, but essential safeguards where friction between a fragment of iron and a combustible powder might lead to an explosion. Respirators, and in some cases veils, are also needful accessories of the filling factory, and these too are provided for the workers.

A complete factory uniform has thus evolved since the war: it is a model of suitable clothing for industrial work. Arising from within the workshops to meet essential needs, these fashions are not only free from vulgarity, or eccentricity, but have a distinct beauty of their own. It is unlikely that women, once accustomed to the comfort and cleanliness of such garments, will desire to return to the discredited habit of tarnished finery worn at work.

Rest-Rooms and First Aid

Ambulance and First-Aid work within the factory was not unusual even in pre-war days. Since the development of munitions production it has become almost a commonplace, and from December 1, 1917, its provision has been obligatory in blast furnaces, foundries, copper-mills, iron-mills, and metal works. Where T.N.T. is handled, the employment of at least one whole-time medical officer is compulsory, if the employees number 2,000, and, if in excess of that figure, at least one additional medical officer must be employed. The professional work of these doctors is supervised by the medical officers of the Welfare and Health Department, who also in a similar way supervise the safety of workers employed upon the manufacture of lethal gases.

The extra expense involved in the provision of such safeguards is by no means unproductive. In one factory, for example, it has been estimated that 2,500 hours were saved in a single week by prompt attention to minor ailments; in another factory, where the firm meets all smaller claims for workmen's compensation, it was found that in a period of eighteen months following the establishment of a First-Aid organization, a credit balance of nearly £500 accrued to the management after all expenses connected with the factory doctor and the nurses had been defrayed.

Tribute should be paid to the medical staff for their share in the triumph of First-Aid work within the munitions factory, for without their extraordinary devotion the record of misadventure would undoubtedly be higher. One hears from time to time how, in a temporary breakdown of such a staff, a single worker will hold the fort. A typical case is recorded in the press as I write. It tells of a young nurse who worked shifts of twenty-four hours at a stretch, for a fortnight, during the absence of her colleagues.

The development of the factory rest-room and cloak-room has also been a marked feature in the munitions factories where women are employed. Formerly, it was usual to see the women workers' outdoor garments hung round the workshop walls; today,(as at time of first publication), in numbers of munitions works, the women's cloak-rooms are provided with cupboards where hot pipes dry wet boots and clothing, where each girl has her own locker with lock and key, and where the maximum of wash-hand basins supplied with hot and cold water are set up. In T.N.T. workshops compulsory washing facilities are even more elaborate. Bath-rooms are available, as well as a generous supply of towels, and face ointment, or powder, are supplied as preventatives to any ill effects from handling explosives.

Inside the workshops the spirit of reform is equally apparent; seats are provided where possible, and lifting-tackle, or sliding boards, are introduced to minimize strain when dealing with heavy weights. Sometimes, one hears how such improvements, suggested for the women employees, are extended to the men. At a certain engineering works, for example, where in pre-war days women had never been employed, it was suggested by a government official that seats should be supplied for the women. The management looked askance. It would be 'such a bad example to the apprentices,' it was said. The point was, however, pressed, and after a short time the suggestion materialized. The manager then stated, with surprised satisfaction, that the seats 'seemed to renew people,' and he had accordingly extended the improvement to the men.

WOMEN POLICE

One of the most recent developments in the protection of women in the factories is the employment of women police. In the summer of 1916, when it was found necessary to obtain further control and supervision of the women employees in munitions works, Sir Edward Henry, the Chief Commissioner of Police, recommended that the Ministry of Munitions should apply to the Women Police Service for a supply of trained women police. This request has now created an extensive development of such work, and today women police are undertaking numerous duties in munitions works. They check the entry of women into the factory; examine passports; search for such contraband as matches, cigarettes, and alcohol; deal with complaints of petty offences; assist the magistrates at the police court, and patrol the neighbourhood of the factory with a view to the protection of the women employed.

As many of the works have been erected in lonely places, and as the shifts are worked by night as well as by day, it can easily be imagined what a safeguard to the young employee is the presence of these female guardians of the peace. Even within the precincts of the factory, the security assured by the patrolling police-women is of great importance, since many of the factories are built on isolated plots extending perhaps six miles from barrier to barrier, and within these boundaries women are often employed in isolated huts, should they be engaged on the production of explosives. The preventive work of the women police is, in these areas, incalculable.

In such ways, welfare work has taken root in the factories of Britain, and in the words of Mr. Lloyd George:

> It is a strange irony, but no small compensation, that the making of weapons of destruction should afford the occasion to humanize industry. Yet such is the case.

SLITTING AND ROUGHING OPTICAL GLASS

VIEW OF CANTEEN KITCHEN

WEIGHING FERROCHROME FOR ANALYSIS

CHAPTER 6

Outside Welfare

RECREATION

The gift in the early days of munitions development of several thousands of pounds from an Indian prince, the Maharajah of Gwalior, for the benefit of munitions employees, helped to focus attention from the outset on their needful recreation. The necessity for a maximum output, bringing in its train long shifts, overtime, and a minimum of holidays, at first left scant leisure at the munition girl's disposal, yet it was at once apparent that some effort must be made to render that leisure healthful and invigorating. As soon as the welfare supervisors took up their positions in the factories and came into living touch with the needs of the women employed, requests found their way to the Ministry of Munitions for grants for recreation purposes from the *maharajah's* fund.

At first, 'a piano for the recreation-room or canteen' was the more general appeal; for, strangely enough, after the long hours in the engineering shops the normal munitions girl craves most, not for passive amusement, such as 'the pictures,' but for free movements of her own body. Above all, she desires to dance, or to enjoy the rhythm of physical drill, or, in the summer, to swim or dive, or to chase a ball in one or other of the popular team games. Within doors, the piano provides, as it were, a spring-board from which she can jump into a leisure-time atmosphere of merriment; it is the send-off to her dance, the guide to her song, and the backbone to the joy found in the united action of physical drill.

The piano once provided in canteen, or recreation-room, you will find the munition girl footing it in the dinner-hour, or tea-interval, or in any other period when she is off duty. So long as the tune be bright, the merry-hearted munition-maker will dance the old dances, or the more complicated modern steps, as her mood suggests.

From self-taught dancing, the desire for a more perfect expression in movement is a natural evolution, and in certain cases grants from the *maharajah's* fund have defrayed the fees of dancing mistress, or sports instructor. Sums from the same source have been paid to assist the organization of a club, for the provision of a recreation-room, for the erection of swings and see-saws, for the installation of a swimming-bath, for tools and seeds for factory girls' gardens, for dramatic entertainments, for lectures for the instruction of apprentices, and in Ireland, for the enlargement of schools for children of women munition workers.

Side by side with these endeavours, other efforts to promote sane amusement for munition makers have been fructifying. Many an enlightened factory employer, studying the problem of woman-labour within his own works, has come to the conclusion that 'if women are called upon to work continuously, especially at repetition jobs, their pleasure in life must be kept alive'. Being business men, they have soon turned the theory into practice, and have encouraged, started, and financed recreation schemes for their own employees.

In Sheffield, for example, successful dramatic entertainments have been given, the actors and actresses emerging from the engineering shops; near Birmingham, a firm has provided a cinema, an orchestra, and a dancing-room for their workpeople, and on Saturday evenings, free conveyance in an omnibus is arranged for those workers resident in outlying hostels and married quarters.

At Norwich, another firm has appointed a woman recreation officer to teach the girls physical drill, dancing, tennis, and other games. Dances and a fancy-dress ball have been organized there, and in the summer, tennis, bowls, and cricket are played in a large recreation ground. These are but a few instances, typical of the growing understanding amongst employers in this country of the value of playtime to a women's staff.

Outside the factory other agencies have been at work, voluntarily attempting to provide rest and refreshment for the women whose sacrifices for the war are so great and so patiently endured. Such bodies as the Young Women's Christian Association or local Civic Associations have opened recreation clubs—sometimes for girls only and sometimes 'mixed'—where concerts, dramatic entertainments, and lectures are given, and classes in useful arts or games are held. Women from the aristocracy and working women, civic authorities and the clergy, have joined hands throughout the country to help forward this effort for the physical, spiritual and intellectual recreation of the munitions worker.

The very spontaneity and eagerness of the movement have naturally led here and there to overlapping, and in the spring of 1917 it was found advisable to co-ordinate local streams of goodwill and energy. A branch of the Welfare and Health Department of the Ministry of Munitions was thus established to keep in touch with all agencies outside the factory which deal with schemes regarding recreation, sickness, maternity-cases, crèches, housing, and transit facilities. Extra-mural welfare officers have since been appointed to undertake such duties in various localities. These act as *liaison* officers between existing associations of every denomination in a given district, and centralize all outside efforts for the protection and relaxation of the munition women of that area.

The welfare officer at first surveys carefully the needs of the district, and institutes an inquiry as to provisions for their satisfaction. If necessary, a conference is then called of individuals and representatives of local bodies dealing with these matters, and sub-committees are appointed for each part of the work. When the numbers of women workers are comparatively small in a given area and no adequate provision has been made for their recreation, a central club is often opened. In other localities, existing clubs, or institutions, are adapted to new requirements, or new ones are added, according to local needs. Where night shifts are worked in the local factories, it is usual to arrange the open hours of the club to suit the workshop leisure hours. Thus, a club may be open from 6 to 8 a.m.; at midday, for two hours, and again from 4.30 to 9.30 p.m. In such cases, it is often necessary to employ paid club managers, as well as local voluntary help.

The clubs, however, vary, both in scope and management, the general principle followed by the welfare officer being to ensure provision for recreation, and then to leave the administration to local effort. Encouragement is given by the Ministry of Munitions to employers of controlled establishments and to the management of national factories to help forward the movement for recreation for their staffs by allowing Treasury grants out of excess profits to be made towards approved schemes. In many districts the grants are 'pooled' for recreation purposes for the whole area. Recreation for the munition worker thus rests on a secure basis. In the winter months, dancing, physical drill, theatricals, games, and classes are in full swing in the principal munitions areas, and in the summer, outdoor sports are encouraged, as well as the tending of vegetable plots and flower gardens.

Motherhood

A more difficult task falling to the 'Outside Welfare' officer is the supervision of maternity cases arising among munition workers. The all-important question of motherhood necessarily crops up in the factories where hundreds of thousands of women are in daily employment. Numbers of them are wives of men hard at work in war industries at home; others are war-widows, and while the illegitimate birth-rate has not gone up disproportionately in munitions areas, the unmarried mother, from time to time, presents a special problem.

The care of the expectant mother necessarily begins within the factory gates. We have so far no published conclusions from an authoritative survey of this question, such as Dr. Bonnaire (Chief Professor of Midwifery at the Maternity Hospital, Paris) has provided for France, yet scientific investigations and experiments undertaken by the Health of Munition Workers' Committee are in progress. As far as possible, the women welfare supervisors within the works keep their management informed of maternity cases as they are noted, and, where possible, the expectant mother is placed on lighter work.

No woman known to be in that condition is, after a certain period, kept on at night work, nor is she allowed to work in an explosives factory, nor yet to handle T.N.T. 'We send the girl to the doctor and we act on his advice. If we can keep her, we always take her off night work and heavy machines and where there is a good deal of exertion,' is a report typical of the procedure in such cases in many factories. 'It is too risky for an expectant mother to stay on at all,' is a characteristic opinion from a filling factory; and from a high-explosives factory comes the verdict that an expectant mother should, after a certain period, be discharged from the works in view of the occasional occurrence there of small explosions. Such maternity cases are, when possible, transferred, through local agencies, to lighter national work outside the factory.

The Factory Nursery

Closely connected with the safeguarding of motherhood is the case of the munition workers' children of pre-school age. After two months' interval from the baby's birth, many of the maternity cases from the factory return to their previous work, and the infant must, in the mother's absence, be nursed by others. A similar condition applies to the work of other mothers whose labour is required for munitions production.

It sometimes happens that in a given area the call to the munitions factories has been answered by practically all the available women in the neighbourhood whose home ties are light, and the local labour reserve is found amongst the women with one or two young children. If these women are to offer their services, it is essential that their young family should not be neglected. Sometimes, the mothers are able to make their own arrangements and a 'minder', either a relative, or a neighbour, is forthcoming, but, generally speaking, such a plan is not satisfactory in a locality where every active individual is undertaking urgent war work.

Thus has arisen in many districts the claim that a nursery for munition workers' children should be established. A local association, or an individual, often finds it possible to finance such a scheme; in other cases, monetary aid is required and obtained from the Ministry of Munitions. In the latter circumstances, the Ministry of Munitions, co-operating with the Board of Education, grants 75 *per cent.* of the approved expenditure on the initial provision and equipment of the nursery, as well as 7*d.* a day for each attendance of a child, the balance of the expenses being met partly by fees (varying from 7*d.* to 1*s.* a day, or from 7*s.* 6*d.* to 9*s.* 6*d.* a week) charged to the mothers, and partly by contributions from the local originators of the scheme.

Where night shifts are worked, the munition workers may claim night accommodation for their children; arrangements are also made to board the infants by the week. In the schemes approved by the ministry it has generally been found possible to adapt existing buildings, but where no suitable accommodation is available within reasonable distance of the mothers' homes a new building is erected.

Such a nursery has been erected near Woolwich and provides a useful model for this country. It is a long low building of bungalow type, surrounded by a small garden. The main room, the babies' parlour, is a long apartment enclosed on two sides by a verandah, and on the third, by a wide passage well ventilated at each end. The room itself is full of light and air, there is plenty of play room, and no awkward corners to inflict bruises unawares. A lengthy crawl brings a baby-boarder into the sunshine of the verandah and the safe seclusion of its playpens, and a longer crawl and a hop is rewarded by entrance into the surrounding garden, where a delectable sand-pit is a permanent feature.

Brightly-coloured flowers enliven the garden in spring and in summer and attract bird and insect visitors, companions often more interesting to a two-year-old than the most sprightly of humans. Mattresses occupy part of the floor space of the nursery, and at night-time are developed into full-fledged beds. At one end of the room are cupboards let into the walls, at the other, furniture fashioned for the needs of each 'two feet nothing.' There, instead of being perched on a high chair to feed with giants from an elevated table-land, the infant visitor sits on a miniature arm-chair at a table brought to the level of childhood. The low tables are, in fact, kidney-shaped and hollowed on the inside, so that a nurse, or attendant, seated in the centre, may feed half a dozen children in turn. The toddler's dinner in this retreat recalls the feeding time in a nest. A smiling nurse in the centre feeds, turn by turn, her open-mouthed charges whose satisfaction is expressed in human 'coos.'

Another room in this delightful babies' house is devoted to infants: a brigade in cots, of which the advance-guard, during fine weather, invade the verandah. The daintiness of the room with its blue curtains and cot-hangings and the chubby satisfaction of the cot-dwellers must be a constant inspiration to the visiting working mothers. Spotless kitchens for the preparation of the children's meals are situated in the rear of the nurseries; there is also an isolation room where suspect infectious cases are detained, and a laundry with an indefatigable laundress. The bathing room, fitted with modern appliances, is in many respects excellent. The whole establishment is warmed by a central-heating installation, the radiators being well protected with guards.

It may not always be possible, through lack of funds, to reproduce these ideal conditions, but where the accommodation is less and the ground space more limited, every care is taken that the factory nursery shall have an ample provision of fresh air. Efforts are also made to obtain as much local support as possible.

In some districts, the whole of the clothing provided at the nursery is made by the little girls from a neighbouring elementary school. At Acton, Middlesex, for example, I was shown piles of the daintiest little underwear, diminutive shoes and charming cotton frocks, all made in the sewing classes at their school, by pupils of eleven to thirteen years of age. The boys of the local manual schools—not to be outdone—contributed to this nursery all the carpentry for the cots for the elder babies. These small beds, fashioned out of hessian cloth, swung on long broom poles, with a wooden board at head and foot, seemed of a particularly economical and practical pattern.

The factory nursery is certainly gaining popularity as a war-time measure; as a permanency in peace times it is recognized that there are some objections to its establishment. An alternative scheme, even in the war period, is being mooted. The suggestion is made that babies should be 'billeted,' or boarded out in the munitions area amongst women who are not employed outside their home. Supervision of the baby boarders, it is thought, might be undertaken by inspectors under the local authority. This scheme might, it is true, largely prevent the congregation of many children in one nursery and the resultant danger of the spread of contagious infantile disease. On the other hand, the proposal, if accepted, might open the doors to overcrowding in thickly populated areas and to the neglect of the baby boarder, undetected by a local inspectorate, already overstrained by war-time conditions. The scheme is, however, only at the discussion stage, as I write.

In any case, the care of the munition workers' children is attracting considerable public attention, since in spite of the war, or because of it, the importance of the health and well-being of the ordinary individual, and more especially of the young, is becoming part of the creed of the average citizen.

CHAPTER 7

Growth of the Industrial Canteen

Money hardly counts; it is labour we have to consider nowadays',
recently remarked the managing director of a large munitions works.
It is this new conception that has given impetus to the development
of the industrial canteen, now a feature of the munitions factory. In
the opinion of Mr. John Hodge, M.P., Minister of Pensions, who since
the war has acted for a long period as Minister of Labour, canteens in
the engineering shops were 'necessary from the start', and one of the
earliest investigations of the Health of Munition Workers' Committee
was on the subject of the provision of employees' meals. The results of
the inquiry are embodied in three valuable White Papers.[1]

I have since been into many canteens connected with munitions
works, and so far I have not met a factory manager who has regret-
ted their introduction. Yet, only three or four years ago, the average
employer would have told you that a dinner brought by a worker in
a newspaper, or tied up in a red handkerchief, stored in the works,
heated anywhere, and eaten near the machines, was 'quite all right:'
and, as for the boys in the factory, it was considered shameful to 'cod-
dle them;' if necessary, a factory lad should 'eat his dinner on a clothes
line.'

Today, when the utmost ounce of energy is needed from man and
woman, and boy and girl, wherever munitions production is concerned, it is recognized that the quality and quantity of the workers'
food matters, and that even the surroundings where the meal is par-

---

1. *Health of Munition Workers Committee*, Memorandum No. 3, Report on Industrial
Canteens (Cd. 8133); Memorandum No. 6, Appendix to Memorandum No. 3, Canteen Construction and Equipment (Cd. 8199); Memorandum No. 19, Investigation
of Workers' Food and Suggestions as to Dietary: Report by Leonard E. Hill, M.B.,
F.R.S. (Cd. 8798).

taken of counts in the conservation of the essential reserve of human energy and power of will. Thus, the best type of industrial canteen is designed not only 'to feed the brute', but to rest his mind. This is especially the case in certain filling factories, where immunity from ill-effects from the handling of T.N.T. has been found to depend largely on the physical fitness of the workers.

In such factories, as well as in establishments where women are employed on night shifts, the provision of canteens is obligatory on employers and, indeed, recent legislation (the Police, Factories, &c. (Miscellaneous Provisions) Act, 1916) has empowered the Home Secretary to require the occupiers of workshops and factories to make arrangements, where necessary, for the supply of meals for their employees. In the stress of warfare, when the demand for a maximum output is necessarily the pre-occupation of the factory manager, it was, however, recognized that the canteen must be State-aided. A Canteen Committee was therefore appointed under the Central Control Board (Liquor Traffic).

The work of this committee is twofold: it aids the factory management to open its own canteen or canteens, and it supervises and helps approved dining-rooms managed by voluntary bodies. In the first case, the expense for any necessary canteen is entirely borne by the government, if the factory is a 'National' one. In controlled establishments, the employer is allowed to charge the cost of the canteen as 'a trade expense,' a concession by which the State practically bears the expense out of funds which would otherwise reach the Exchequer. In the case of canteens provided by voluntary bodies, such as the Young Men's Christian Association, the Young Women's Christian Association, the Church Army, the Salvation Army, the National People's Palace Association, Ltd., &c., the Board pays half the capital expenditure, where approved.[2]

The efforts of these voluntary bodies have been of the utmost service, especially at the outset of munitions production on a vast scale, when the factory proprietors, or directors, were unable to devote even a fraction of their time to matters not obviously connected with output. The devotion of the unpaid workers in the voluntary canteen has through the turmoil of war hardly received due recognition, but it is no less than that of the nurses in the military hospitals, or of the munitions workers themselves. Women of aristocratic families, accustomed

---

2. A Food Section of the Ministry of Munitions has since been established to carry on the work of the Central Control Board (Liquor Traffic).

BALSMING LENSES

MAKING INSTRUMENT SCALES

to personal service from a large staff of domestic servants, and entirely unused to physical labour, as well as women hard-worked in their own homes or in livelihood occupations, have, since the need of the canteen was declared, come, by day and by night, to undertake the arduous duties of cooking and scrubbing for vast numbers of working-people. *Mr. Punch's* delightful illustration, 'War, the Leveller,' where the rough scullery-maid from the slums is depicted issuing the emphatic order to the well-bred marchioness, 'Nah then, Lady Montgummery Wilberforce, 'urry up with them plates,'[3] is by no means a fancy picture of the hither side of canteen-life.

In one factory, substantial meals have been provided daily by 17 voluntary assistants for some 1,200 workers; in another locality, the food of 2,000 to 3,000 munitions employees has been arranged by 23 volunteers; and in another establishment, 6,000 workers have been provided with standing-up refreshments by 17 voluntary helpers. The rapid growth of the canteen system during the past fifteen months, accompanied by the increasing difficulties of catering for vast numbers under war-time conditions, has, however, led to the transference of numbers of voluntary canteens to the care of the factory management.

GENERAL PRINCIPLES

Industrial canteens differ from one another in many respects, partly because there was at first no fund of common experience in this country from which to draw, and partly because hours of work, tastes and customs in industrial areas vary considerably. Hence, methods of administration and catering, found possible or popular in one canteen, are sometimes a complete failure when tried in other districts. In one canteen, with a seating capacity for 2,000 women, I found that three gallons of pickles were sold in pennyworths daily; in another district, the popular taste ran in the direction of jam tarts. Yet, even with the small store of experience so far accumulated, certain general principles at least as regards site, construction, equipment, and administration of the canteen have been evolved. For instance, as regards site, a gloomy dining-room is never popular. If possible, a garden outlook should be arranged, and at the least, the canteen walls should be of a restful colour. It seems obvious that if pictures are introduced, they should be varied and bright, yet I have seen one canteen of which the walls were covered at intervals with reproductions of the same

---

3. *Punch*, September 6, 1916.

uninteresting print.

Another obvious point, too often neglected, is the insurance of good ventilation in canteen and kitchen. The dining-room should, if possible, provide separate accommodation for men and women, and should have a buffet-bar and serving-counter with separate hatchments for different items of the menu. Again, it is a matter of common consent that the 'ticket system' of payment for the food handed over the counter is the best. Ticket-offices, where the 'checks' are obtainable for cash, should be carefully placed with regard to entrance doors, serving-counters and dining-tables, so that the minimum time is expended in preliminaries by a *clientèle* who has but a strict dinner-hour at its disposal. In a well-organized canteen I have seen over a thousand workers seated and served within ten minutes of the announcement of the dinner-hour within the factory shops.

In the larger canteens, developments, as may be expected, run chiefly along the lines of labour-saving appliances. Electric washing-up machines, electric bacon-cutters, as well as electric bread-cutters, tea-measuring machines, counter hot-closets for warming food brought by employees may now be seen in many kitchens where the needs of thousands of diners must be considered.

But it is perhaps in the smaller concerns that the development of the industrial canteen is most assured. Experiments can there be more easily tried, and if necessary, discarded, where the customers are counted by hundreds, rather than by thousands. From a tour of canteens, I select a couple of such instances. The other day I happened, during the dinner-hour, to be in a new munitions factory concerned with the production of magnetos, aero-engines, electric switches, and so on, work undertaken by men and women, boys and girls. The manager of this works has studied the labour question up and down the country, and has set down his conclusions, not on minute sheets, but in the bricks and mortar of new buildings, in green lawns and flower beds bright with colour, and in allotments round his shops.

THE WORKER'S OASIS

The canteen is a feature of the place. It stands apart from the factory, a long low building, one side looking on to a tennis court and the other on to homely but delightful vegetable plots. The workers' dining-room is divided down the centre: one side for the men, the other for the women. A serving-table, but no partition-wall, separates it from the kitchen, which, in its turn, is divided by further serving-tables from mess-rooms for the engineers and staff employees. The kitchen, in reality a series of ovens, stoves, and steamers, is a revelation of labour-saving appliances, heated by electricity. On the day of my visit there was not the slightest odour of cooking from these various utensils, although hot meals for some 250 persons were in preparation.

The factory hooter 'buzzed'. The dinner hour, the workers' oasis, had arrived, yet there was no clatter of dishes, or bustle of serving-maids, in the canteens. An atmosphere of repose was as manifest as in a well-appointed reception-room of some stately English home. The workers evidently react to these conditions, and standing at the back of the kitchen I was quite unaware of the diner's entry.

'When do the people come in?' I asked from my shelter behind a huge steamer where puddings were rising to the occasion.

'A hundred men are already seated and served', was the amazing reply. They had entered through a side door leading out of the garden, had there purchased a 'check' for the value of the dinner required, and presenting the 'check' at the serving-counter, had received their portion, piping hot from the hot shelves fitted beneath.

Picking up the necessary cutlery from an adjoining table, the customers had seated themselves at any special small marble-topped table of their fancy. Waitresses, some voluntary workers garbed in rose-coloured overalls and mob-caps, and some staff employees in white or blue uniforms, moved about amongst the tables, supplying small wants. Through the open windows floated the scent of hay and flowers; it seemed almost ludicrous to connect the scene with war and the manufacture of its engines of destruction. The quality of the food was excellent and the variety great. A dinner hour spent in such a canteen is a refreshment to both body and soul of the employees.

In another instance, the firm have handed over the canteen and its management to a workers' committee upon which the managing director also sits. I noticed in this canteen various devices worthy of imitation, where catering is undertaken for large numbers. The method adopted, for example, of dividing the serving-counter into hatchments for the various items on the menu, and separating by rails the floor-space in front of each compartment, seems to economize both the time and patience of the customers. The note of economy with efficiency is emphasized in this, as in many canteens, and I was shown with pride some 'little brothers' on an adjoining piece of land—pigs that were fattening on the canteen 'waste'.

These developments, started in munitions areas during the urgency of warfare, will, without doubt, have permanent importance in the days of peace, and it is probable that the munition workers' canteen, doubtingly adopted by employers some two years ago, is symptomatic of a revolution in the home life of the industrial worker, as well as of new methods of economy in the national supply of fuel and food.

CHAPTER 8

Housing

Of the indirect problems arising from a prolific output of munitions the most acute has undoubtedly been the affair of the housing of the workers. The opening of a new factory, or the conversion of existing works to the needs of the State, often involve the transference of thousands of workers, and in some cases the districts to which the stream of immigration is directed are already congested, and already suffering from inadequate housing accommodation.

In one town in the North, for example, the population has since 1914 increased by immigration from 16,000 to 35,000; in another town, where the 1911 census showed a population of 107,821, an un-exaggerated estimate gives the figure for the end of 1917 as 120,000; in other munition areas a similar inflation of population has taken place. The housing problem has been further complicated by the al-most total prohibition of building during the war period, save for government purposes.

The effect of these conditions in the early days of the war was, as may be imagined, highly unsatisfactory to the residents in certain munition areas, as well as to the immigrant work-people. Overcrowding became rife; lodgers were at the mercy of unscrupulous landladies, and all the evils associated with bad housing conditions began to make their appearance. Then the Ministry of Munitions came to grips with the question, and although it remains a thorny subject, the activities of the department may be fairly said to have accomplished a miracle in some areas in the housing of the munition workers.

The infinite variety of local conditions, as well as the humanness of the workers, obviously complicate the matter, and while it has been found possible to synthesize the factory system of a given area, no ster-eotyped regulations can conceivably be produced to cover the accommodation of its employees. The problem is therefore attacked piece-meal, each local proposition being decided on its own merits. A broad guiding principle has, however, been educed wherever the housing situation occasioned by the output of munitions demands State inter-vention. In the first place, it is decided whether the needed accommo-dation can be met in part, or altogether, by existing houses—a system now sanctioned by the Billeting Act of May 1917. Secondly, when it is found necessary to provide further housing room, consideration is given as to whether new buildings shall be of a temporary or of a permanent type.

BILLETING

Chronologically, an authorized system of billeting munition work-ers has been the latest development in the State housing schemes, but even in the early days of the war this arrangement existed in embryo. Local committees were then appointed which, with the aid of the Employment Bureaux, compiled lists of suitable lodgings for immigrant women workers. From the earliest war period, too, provi-sion was made to meet young women new-comers at railway stations and to place them, if necessary, in temporary unimpeachable lodgings, until permanent accommodation was available. This scheme has now developed into the regularized activities of a Billeting Board (estab-lished August 1917), working under powers given by the Billeting Act. Under this enactment, compulsory billeting is provided for, but in practice is not adopted, sufficient facilities having so far been forth-coming from voluntary sources.

The Billeting Board works in hearty co-operation with local au-thorities and individuals, and has met with extraordinary success. In the first instance, two executive members of the Board proceed to a congested munitions area and, with local aid, institute an inquiry as to whether billeting can be successfully carried out. In such areas as the Clyde, or Woolwich, billeting would, for example, be out of the question, but in other localities, such as Barrow and Hereford, where public opinion ran that there was no further accommodation even for a stray cat, the Board has yet found suitable billets for 900 persons in Barrow and 1,200 in Hereford.

The question of transit, it is true, is intimately connected with the housing problem, and through the action of the Billeting Board it has in many cases been possible to remove difficulties of locomotion, and hence to bring further accommodation within reach of the factories.

The Board has also been enabled to form local committees on which sit representatives of each housing interest (e. g. landlady, locality, lodger), and it has authority to recover rent from defaulting tenants.

These, and other powers, have resulted in throwing many additional apartments on to the market. Yet difficulties remain in the administration of the Act in that the industrial workers are under no discipline such as that applied to soldiers, and there is no local authority to compel a munitions worker either to go into a given billet, or to remain there when placed. The goodwill of the locality and of the employees has, however, been so great that the system works smoothly, and from August 1917 to December 31, 1917, 3,000 to 5,000 munition workers have been placed in existing houses. In a congested district where lodging accommodation is exhausted, the Billeting Board reports on the need for further houses, and at such centres as Barrow and Lincoln new houses are now being erected on their recommendation.

TEMPORARY ACCOMMODATION

Excluding the utilization of local lodgings and the adaptation of existing buildings such as Poor-Law structures, Elementary Schools, charitable institutions, three distinct types of provisional accommodation for munition workers have made their appearance: temporary cottages, hostels, and colonies. The temporary cottage corresponds fairly closely to the ordinary type of permanent industrial cottage, save that the former is built of wood or concrete and is usually one story instead of two; it contains three to five rooms, and is rented on the basis of about 5s .6d. to 7s. 6d. per week for a three-roomed abode.

Generally speaking, these rooms are allocated to married rather than to single women; sometimes the wife, as well as the husband, works in the neighbouring factory, but more usually the wife, housed in the temporary cottage, remains at home, housekeeping for the man worker. The unmarried girls and women workers in crowded districts are generally accommodated in hostels, or in colonies, the term used for a group of hostels. The hostel, which is designed to accommodate from 30 to 100 persons, is provided with its own kitchen, dining-room, and common-room, and to a certain extent life therein approximates to that of a large family.

The colony, or group of hostels, has been found convenient where a large number of women must be housed. Each hostel, or hutment, in the group is arranged for the sleeping accommodation of 100-130 persons, the dormitories being divided into cubicles (some single, some double), accommodation for bathrooms being always made in these dormitory blocks. Under the colony system, meals are usually partaken of in a separate building or buildings. The residents from all the hutments also meet in the recreation-room and in the laundry, common to all.

Experience, however, teaches that each hostel should have its own common room and that a colony should not shelter very large numbers. About 500 girls, in five hostels, seems to be the ideal number for effective home-making, yet we have large housing schemes for the accommodation of many thousands which are at present answering their purpose as a war-time measure. For the management of the colony an exceptionally capable lady superintendent is needed, into whose hands usually falls the selection of the hutment matrons and their staffs, as well as the canteen managers and their subordinates. In the most developed colonies a recreation officer is often appointed.

I recall a visit to one of the largest colonies for munition workers in the Midlands. The scheme embraces the housing and feeding of some 6,000 women, drawn from every part of the United Kingdom, indeed, possibly from every corner of the Empire. The staff, in all, comprises some 300 persons. Perfect harmony reigned, and the girls seemed thoroughly at home in their novel surroundings. Each girl can claim a separate cubicle, which is divided from the adjoining compartment by a wall and door. Here and there, indeed, the arrangement was varied and two friends—terrified at sleeping alone—had secured permission to pool their bedrooms and to arrange a double sleeping-room and dressing-room.

The cubicle system is, notwithstanding, much appreciated by the woman, who, working in company of hundreds of her fellows, and sharing perhaps a common life for the first time, rejoices in the possession of some spot in which to express her inner self. In some cubicles in that colony a desire for beauty asserted itself and the walls were gay with prints from illustrated papers; in others, dainty coloured curtains had been introduced and the locker was covered with a cloth to match. In another room, the owner had evidently a taste for embroidery, and all the toilet accessories bore this feminine touch. But, generally speaking, the chief feature I noticed in that, as well as in other colonies where the cubicle system prevails, was the cleanliness and order of the apartments. A taste for purity is infectious, and it is unlikely that girls, having once come under an influence that induces them to leave their sleeping apartment immaculate before going to work before dawn, will ever again tolerate slum conditions.

The many problems involved in the housing of these girls of various types are indeed almost lost sight of by the visitor, but, as a lady superintendent once reminded me, there are difficulties inherent in the job. Some girls will arrive with uncleanly habits, even when the medical officer has sorted out those unclean in person; others will, at first, show signs of violent antipathies and strange fears, and there is always the need for upholding an atmosphere of religious and racial toleration. In the Midlands colony a system has been adopted of placing the bedrooms of girls from one part of the United Kingdom in the same corridor, the Irish in one wing, the Scotch in another, and so on, but in the other parts of the country I have found perfect harmony where such classification is not observed.

The feeding of the hostel residents presents its own difficulties, especially in these days of war. In some hostels and colonies, such as the one in the Midlands, the residents take their meals in their own canteen; it being possible to supply the needs of a shift in the interval from work. In other hostels, arrangements are made by which meals can be had either at the hostel or the factory canteen.

In these days of fluctuating food prices, it is difficult to indicate the cost of upkeep of a munition-workers' hostel, but, in general, it has not been found practicable to put the hostel on an entirely self-supporting basis. This is especially the case in the government establishments, where the return on expended capital is at present only sought in increased munitions output.

PERMANENT ACCOMMODATION

At first sight, the provision of temporary accommodation alone may appear the obvious method for the housing of munition workers. Cheaper and more rapid construction is obtainable by this method, and existing buildings may be adapted. But if, in an area of pre-war housing shortage, there is good prospect of permanent manufacturing activity, it is more often decided that permanent, rather than temporary, structures are provided.

It may be of interest to note the methods that have been adopted by the State in the provision of permanent accommodation. These may be detailed under four heads:

1. In a certain number of cases loans have been made to Public Utility Societies for the construction of dwellings for munition workers. Such loans are conditioned after the manner already

PAINTING A SHIP'S SIDE IN DRY DOCK

GENERAL VIEW OF WOMEN AT WORK ON AIRCRAFT FABRIC

THE CANTEEN

made familiar to the public by Garden Suburb and other Associations.

2. Loans have been made directly to certain individual firms to enable them to house their immigrant employees. These loans have been issued at the current rate of interest—usually 5 *per cent.*—and run, generally speaking, for a period of forty years.

3. In a few exceptional cases, certain private firms—now controlled establishments—are permitted to charge a part of the increase on the cost of building (due to war conditions) to that portion of the firm's profits which would otherwise have gone to the Exchequer.

4. A contribution is, in some instances, made by the State to certain local authorities of a part of the capital cost of building. In all cases this contribution is less than the estimated increase due to war conditions.

The type of permanent building erected by such means is that which characterizes many of our newer industrial districts, namely a two-story brick cottage, containing two or three bedrooms, a living-room and a kitchen, a bath, in some cases a bathroom. Sometimes a complete village or township has arisen, as it were from the earth, to shelter the working population who have so willingly left their homes to further the common cause by land and sea. In another instance, a large national factory has been erected on an isolated waste in the North country. The workers come from long distances, and not only need accommodation, but some reasonable provision for recreation and the amenities of life.

Beyond the great high road sweeping on to Scotland, some one- or two-roomed cottages, a village shop or two, and a few more imposing residences there was, in June 1915, nothing but bogland in the immediate neighbourhood of the site of this new factory. The landscape presented a view of coarse grass and brackish water; beyond that, beach and sea, and a horizon bounded by rugged mountains, capped in winter by snow. It needed courage, as well as genius, to undertake the transformation of such a desolate waste into surroundings which should offer a lure to industrial workers. But the work has been done in silence, quickly as well as efficiently, with imagination, as well as thoroughness, and with an eye to the future destiny of the place.

By July 1915, the first huts were occupied, and by December 1917, when I was a privileged visitor, there had arisen a thriving busy township and a village some five miles beyond. Excellent railway communication between township, village, and factory has been established, many good roads have been built, there are permanent cottages, churches, a school, shops, a staff club, an institute, a large entertainment hall, a cinema house, and a central kitchen, providing cooked meals for all the workers in the factories, and raw food-stuff for hostels and huts. Little gardens surround the houses big and small, temporary or permanent, and allotments are in great request, and there is also provision for outdoor recreation, such as bowls, tennis, cricket, &c. The permanent brick cottages are built in blocks of twelve, which are now thrown together to form a hostel. The construction is so planned that ultimately these cottages can be re-separated for family use.

There is housing accommodation for over 6,000 women operators, which was practically all in use. The task of supervising the home conditions of this army of women falls into the hands of a lady welfare superintendent, who keeps all the complicated machinery of hostels, huts, and lodgings in running order. The possibilities in the housing of industrial women away from their own homes have, I believe, never been so clearly demonstrated as in this town on the marshes. The lady superintendent who has pioneered this movement is of the opinion that its success is bound up with the fact that the hostels are limited to the accommodation of from 70 to 100 girls in each. Other key-notes to the prevailing happiness of the women residents are, I gathered, that a minimum number of rules are enforced and that the women are treated as responsible human beings. The elder women are often housed in bungalows under the care of a housekeeper-cook, and they greatly enjoy the greater independence and the appeal to their individuality possible in such surroundings.

The hostels, at the time of my visit, were in most hospitable mood. It was the eve of Christmas, and festivities, tempered to war-time needs, were the order of the day. The sound of a piano and singing outside a certain hostel suggested a frolic within. We entered, the lady superintendent and myself. The lower floor had been converted into reception-rooms and supper was laid out on tables decorated with spoils from the hedge. Gleaming red berries and glistening holly-leaves were on walls and brackets and here and there a sprig of mistletoe placed in suitable places for 'auld lang syne.' There were present young men, as well as girls, and a lively game, 'the Duke of York,' was in progress.

Suddenly the singing and accompaniment came to a sudden halt and the whole of the company trouped in from adjoining rooms. A young girl came forward. 'We wish to take this opportunity', she said, 'of thanking our matron and our secretary for the most happy time we have had under this roof. We do it now because we hope not to be here next year, but instead to be welcoming our boys home from the Front'. It was a simple, spontaneous expression of the general emotion of the hostel residents in that area.

Everywhere I found a similar joy of life among the workers: in the Institute clubs, where both girls and men were reading, studying, singing, and dancing; in the cinema hall, where the ever-popular 'movies' were taking place; and in the big recreation hall, where a weekly 'social' was being held. There, two girls provided the band, to which other girls danced with girls, or with men in khaki, or with factory workers in civilian dress. There was a healthy comradeship between girls and men and, when the hour of parting came there were leave-takings of which no one could be ashamed. Laughter and jollity in plenty, and snatches of song up and down the darkened streets, as group after group found its way home, but self-respect and dignity noticeably present.

In a new town, emerging during the hurry and bustle of the war, amongst new occupations, at which women needs must wear a masculine costume, we have at least accomplished this: that the spirit of home-life, of joy, and of love has not been discouraged: rather has it been fostered, or rekindled, in these unaccustomed homes provided by the State. Indeed, many of the girls passing through this strange wartime adventure have assuredly gained by their pilgrimage precisely in those qualities most needed by the wives and mothers of the rising generation.

It was an inspiring glimpse into a new industrial world, a portent, maybe, of the time to come. The words of a golden sonnet welled up:

Then felt I like some watcher of the skies
When a new planet swims into his ken;
Or like stout Cortez when, with eagle eyes,
He stared at the Pacific—and all his men
Looked at each other with a wild surmise—
Silent, upon a peak in Darien.

Carry On: British Women's Work in Wartime

Foreword

It is no exaggeration, but the most sober truth, to say that but for the women of Britain and their work, Germany would by now have won the war. For had they failed to rise to the unprecedented demands which their country has made upon them, Britain's industrial effort would have collapsed, and her armies in the field would have been paralyzed. Some three million men have been withdrawn from British industry to serve with the colours; 25 *per cent*, of the male labour employed in the chemical and engineering trades has been drafted into the army; the normal staffs of offices, factories, railways and munition shops have been stripped to the bone at the imperious call of war. Had the women of Britain been unable or unwilling to step into the vacant places, the war, first lost in the workshop, would have been finally lost in the field.

But the women of Britain have not failed. Rather, they have taken up their unlooked-for task with an energy, an enthusiasm and an efficiency which have been one of the miracles of history. Today, (as at time of first publication), there are some 900,000 British women engaged in war industries, and of these more than 600,000 are directly employed on the manufacture of munitions. In shipyards and in iron foundries, in chemical and engineering works, they are ceaselessly working by day and night. Eighteen months ago two-thirds of the 500 processes in the making of munitions on which they are now engaged had never been performed by a woman. The women of Britain are putting over the barrage, without which their sons, their husbands and their brothers could never hope to shatter the German lines.

But it is not in munition work alone that the face of British industry has been transformed by the extension of women labour. As post-women and police, as bakers and farm workers, as motor drivers and 'bus conductors—in almost every occupation of which the mind can think—British women are now cheerfully "carrying on" while their menfolk are away. In her hour of greatest need Britain has called to her daughters. She has not called in vain. By their industry, their efforts and their heroic sacrifice, the women of Britain have saved their country and saved the world.

WOMEN'S WORK FOR THE NAVY: A SCENE IN A SHIPBUILDING YARD

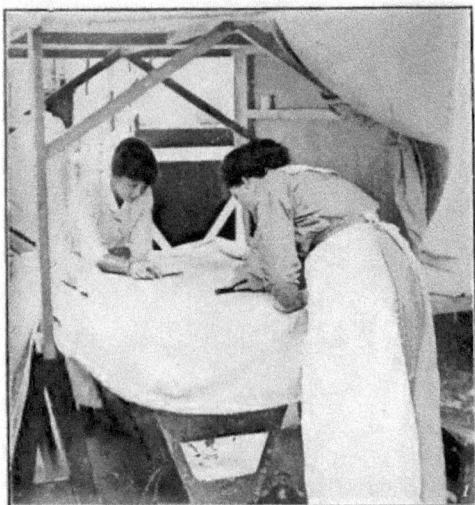

WOMEN AT WORK IN AN AIRCRAFT FACTORY.—
1. INSPECTING AIRCRAFT FABRIC SEAMS.
2. A GENERAL VIEW OF THE FACTORY.

3. TESTING ELECTRIC AIRCRAFT INSTRUMENTS.
4. MAKING SEAPLANE FLOATS.
5. A VIEW OF THE DOPE ROOM.

WOMEN AT WORK ON 9.2-IN. HIGH-EXPLOSIVE SHELLS.—1. FITTING AND
SCREWING THE NOSE-BUSH OF A SHELL. 2. INSPECTING A SHELL.
3. ROUGH-FUMING A SHELL.

HELPING THE BOYS AT THE FRONT—1. WOMEN COPPER-BANDING
60-PDR. SHRAPNEL. 2. WOMEN BAGGING T.N.T.

HELPING THE BOYS ON SEA AND LAND.—1. WOMEN WORKING ON CONDENSERS
FOR MARINE ENGINES. 2. WOMEN PUNCHING ANGLES FOR TRENCH-SHELTERS.

HELPING THE BOYS AT THE FRONT: A WOMAN BORING WOODEN REELS FOR WINDING BARBED WIRE

HEAVY TASKS PERFORMED BY WOMEN WORKERS—1. LABOURING WORK IN A
DRESSING-SHOP. 2. LOADING NITRATE OF SODA INTO A SKIP.

3. CLEARING EARTH EXCAVATED FOR THE INSTALLATION OF HYDRAULIC
PUMPS. 4. A WOMAN STOKER. 5. WHEELING SPENT OXIDE.

BRITISH WOMEN ENGAGED ON WAR WORK. 1. A WOMAN IN CHARGE OF AN
ELECTRIC MOTOR. 2. WOMEN MACHINING ADMIRALTY ELECTRICAL FITTINGS.

A HIVE OF INDUSTRY: WOMEN AT WORK IN A BRASS-FITTING SHOP

BRITISH WOMEN AT WORK ON THE LAND.—
1. FOLLOWING THE HARROW. 2. BRINGING HOME THE CATTLE

3. Loading hay. 4. Ploughing a potato field.

WOMEN AT WORK ON THE FARM.—1. RINGING THE PIG. 2. FEEDING THE PIGS.

WOMEN BAKERS AT WORK—1. TAKING THE BREAD FROM THE OVEN. 2.
LOADING UP THE DELIVERY VAN.

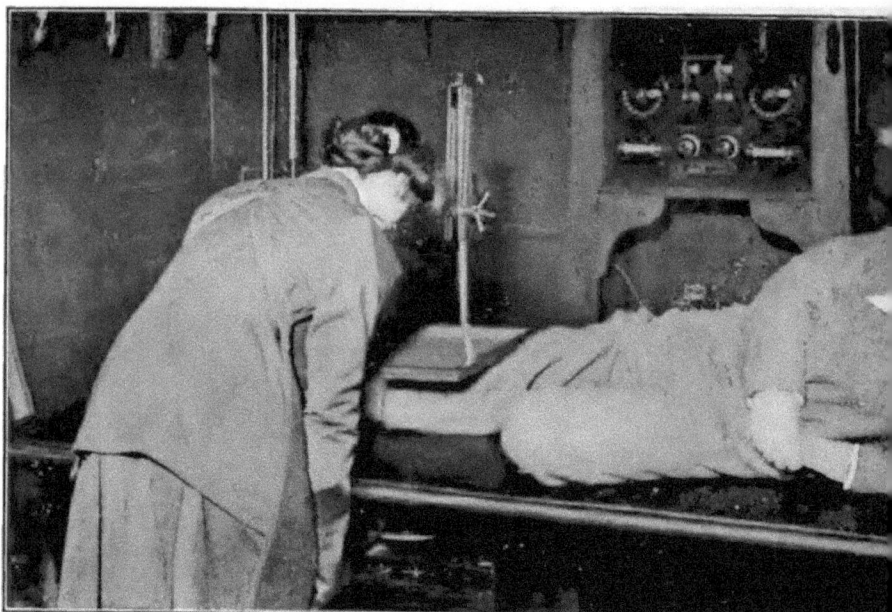

WOMEN ENGAGED IN HOSPITAL AND AMBULANCE WORK.—1. AN X-RAY EXAMINATION.

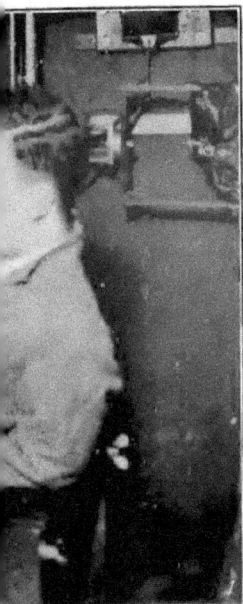

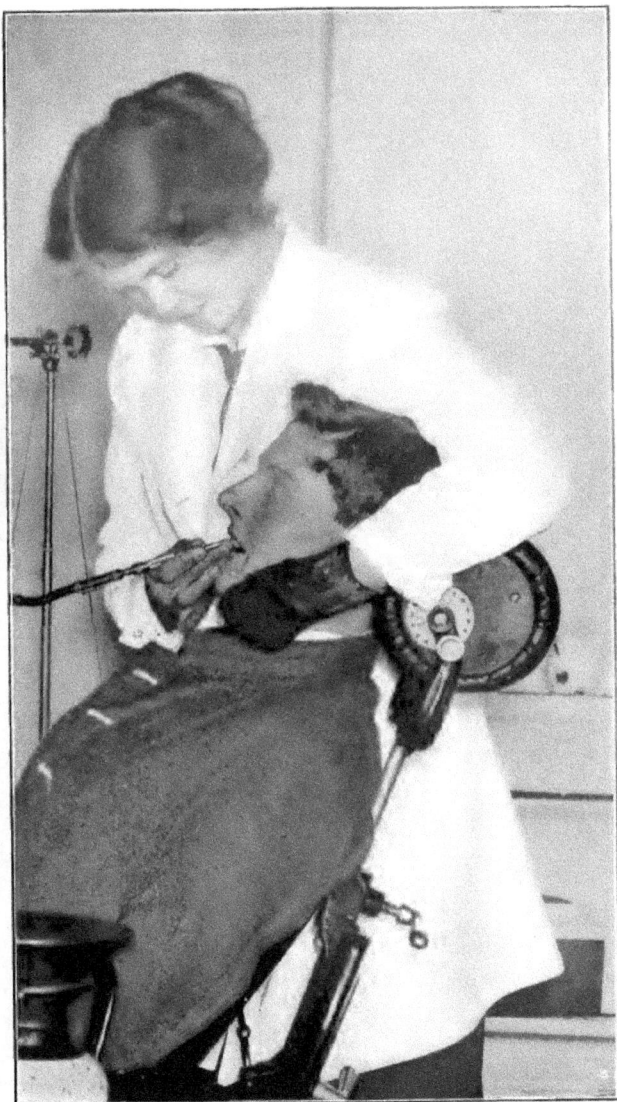

. A Red Cross ambulance. 3. In the pathology laboratory. 4. A lady dentist.

ON THE RAILWAYS: WOMEN CLEANERS AND GREASERS.

WOMEN WINDOW-CLEANERS AT WORK.—1. STARTING OUT ON THEIR
ROUNDS. 2. COMMENCING THE OPERATIONS.

"CARRYING ON" WHILE THE MEN ARE AWAY.—1. WOMEN MOTOR-DRIVERS. 2. A BUS CONDUCTRESS. 3. SOME OF LONDON'S POSTWOMEN.

"CARRYING ON." WHILE THE MEN ARE AWAY.—1. WOMEN PAINTING WAR OF-
FICE VEHICLES. 2. WOMEN ROAD-WORKERS IN A LONDON SUBURB.

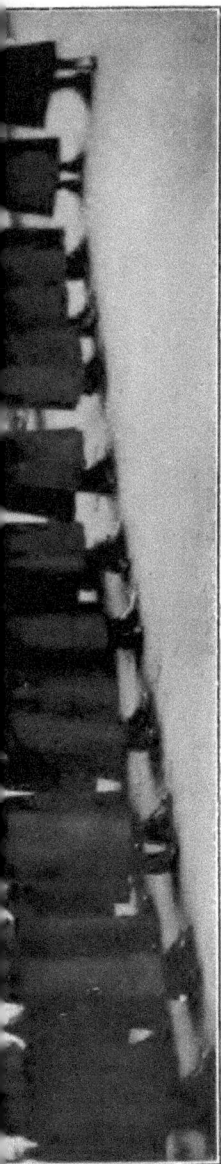

A MISCELLANY OF WOMEN WORKERS. 1. STABLE HELPERS AT A CONVALESCENT REMOUNT DEPOT. 2. A LOCK-KEEPER ON THE THAMES. 3. THE LONDON WOMEN'S POLICE FORCE. 4. THE VILLAGE BLACKSMITH.

AT A BIG LONDON SHOP: A WOMAN COMMISSIONAIRE.